KRAV MAGA DEFENSE

CALGARY PUBLIC LIBRARY

NOV   2016

ALSO BY DAVID KAHN

Krav Maga: An Essential Guide to the Renowned Method—for Fitness and Self-Defense

Advanced Krav Maga: The Next Level of Fitness and Self-Defense

KRAV MAGA DEFENSE

HOW TO DEFEND YOURSELF AGAINST THE 12

MOST COMMON UNARMED STREET ATTACKS

DAVID KAHN

St. MARTIN'S GRIFFIN 🦁 NEW YORK

Nothing contained herein is intended to provide or present any type of legal counsel or advice. Seek counsel from an attorney or use-of-force subject matter expert regarding the self-defense laws applicable to you. This material is intended for educational purposes only. The reader assumes all risk in practicing the strategies and tactics described directly or indirectly in this book. St. Martin's Press and the author disclaim any and all legal liability that may result from the use of this material in any venue whatsoever.

KRAV MAGA DEFENSE. Copyright © 2016 by David Kahn. All rights reserved. Printed in the United States of America. For information, address St. Martin's Press, 175 Fifth Avenue, New York, N.Y. 10010.

www.stmartins.com

Book design by Richard Oriolo
Photographs by Mimi Rowland and Rinaldo Rossi
Cover photograph by Rinaldo Rossi

Library of Congress Cataloging-in-Publication Data

Names: Kahn, David, 1972–
Title: Krav Maga defense : how to defend yourself against the 12 most common unarmed
    street attacks / David Kahn.
Description: First Edition. | New York : St. Martin's Griffin, [2016]
Identifiers: LCCN 2016003971| ISBN 9781250090829 (trade paperback) | ISBN
    9781250090836 (e-book)
Subjects: LCSH: Krav maga.
Classification: LCC GV1111 .K34 2016 | DDC 796.81—dc23
LC record available at http://lccn.loc.gov/2016003971

Our books may be purchased in bulk for promotional, educational, or business use. Please contact your local bookseller or the Macmillan Corporate and Premium Sales Department at 1-800-221-7945, extension 5442, or by e-mail at MacmillanSpecialMarkets@macmillan.com.

FIRST EDITION: June 2016

10 9 8 7 6 5 4 3 2 1

For Claire, Benjamin, and Leo

In Memory of Al Blitstein, who stormed Omaha Beach in WW II
to help liberate Europe, was Imi Lichtenfeld's friend, and was
one of krav maga's greatest friends. He is missed.

CONTENTS

ACKNOWLEDGMENTS

I AM INDEBTED TO GRANDMASTER HAIM GIDON for instilling in me the self-defense fighting style of krav maga at its highest and most evolved level. As the head of the Israeli krav maga system and president of the Israeli Krav Maga Association (IKMA) Gidon System, Haim continues to develop and improve the krav maga system on a daily basis. With the blessing of Imi Lichtenfeld (the late founder of krav maga), Haim, along with the most capable assistance and expert insight from his sons (Albert, Ohad, and Noam) and other senior IKMA instructors, represent the vanguard of krav maga development. Haim emphasizes that the krav maga we teach must work against determined and concerted resistance, against someone who knows how to attack. I can only hope that I can adequately represent Haim's unparalleled krav maga mastery. The quote from Charles Caleb Colton comes to mind: "Imitation is the sincerest form of flattery."

The IKMA board of directors and all IKMA members who continue to welcome and train with me over the years deserve special recognition. This book would not be possible without the expert training, support, and inspiration of krav maga's backbone: the IKMA (www.kravmagaisraeli.com).

Sergeant Major Reserve (Res.) Nir Maman, former LOTAR lead counterterror and krav maga instructor and 2009's IDF Ground Forces Infantry and Paratroopers Command Soldier of the Year, has improved the Israeli krav maga system as only he can with his unique professional insights, specialized training expertise, and great support. Nir is also one of my greatest friends.

I am grateful to my other Israeli krav maga instructors and close friends. Yoav Krayn is not only instrumental to my krav maga development, but he is a superb friend, and also a mentor concerning life's triumphs and tribulations. Another wonderful friend, Aldema Tzrinksky, has provided immeasurable support and counsel over our many years of friendship. I am grateful to the Hauerstocks for their sabra hospitality in my biannual visits to Israel and to my good friend Shira Orbas, now one of the best in the security "business," along with her wonderful family. I offer special thanks to Master Kobi Lichtenstein and the South American Federation for Krav Maga for their hospitality.

Heartfelt thanks also goes to instructor Rinaldo Rossi for both being in front of and behind the lens, along with Chris Eckel and Don Melnick for their collective instructional and unparalleled support. Rinaldo is truly one of the world's foremost krav maga instructors and black-belt practitioners. This book would not exist without Rinaldo's dedication, patience, and generosity, along with the respective help of Don and Chris. They are true brothers to me, embodying the greatest dedication, entrepreneurial spirit, work ethic, and loyalty. Instructor Mimi Rowland performed a near miraculous feat in helping to organize the multitude of photos, along with her creativity in shooting them. Thank you, Mimi. I am grateful to Jason Weber for his friendship, support, sponsorship, and commiseration!

Yet again, this book would not exist without senior krav maga instructors Rick Blitstein and Alan Feldman, who are support strongholds and knowledge reservoirs. Moreover, Rick and Alan brought krav maga to the United States in 1981. Their collective wisdom inspires me to improve as an instructor. Our good friend in Poland, Kris Sawicki, maintains the IKMA at the forefront in Europe.

It is an honor and privilege to work with my great friend Major (Ret.) H. C. "Sparky" Bollinger. I first met Sparky at Camp Lejeune, North Carolina, through an introduction of our mutual friend Captain (Ret.) Frank Small. Frank invited us to teach select Marines at Camp Lejeune and persuaded Sparky, fresh off a flight from the Helmand Province in Afghanistan after his second tour of duty, to attend the training. I knew right away that Sparky was a pro when it came to martial arts training. We were very appreciative of Sparky's acceptance and recognition that our krav maga "was good to go." Hence, a great friendship along with a mutual learning curve developed. He is a true comrade.

Frank Small is not only a close friend, he is also a business partner and founder of Warrior Elite Systems, LLC. Frank spearheaded our instructors' ability to work with the U.S. military. I am also grateful to Frank's wonderful wife, Dana. Frank quickly grasped the paramount importance of professional training: implementing only those tactics that work against concerted resistance. With this mind-set he has paved the way to working with some of the finest professional warriors in America including Master Sergeant Ronald E. Jacobs, former chief instructor of the U.S. Marine Corps Martial Arts Program (MCMAP). Ron holds a sixth-degree black belt in MCMAP, along with numerous other high-ranking belts in other martial arts systems, including a black belt in Israeli krav maga. It is both an honor and privilege to work with Ron; he is a consummate professional and a great friend. I am obliged to Navy instructors S. R., J. N., and J. along with Commander A.L. for their unequaled professional insights, hospitality, and, most importantly, for what they and their colleagues do.

I give thanks to A. B. Duki and Marc of the Residence Beach Hotel (www.zyvotels .com) for hosting our biannual training stays in Netanya, Israel. A. J. Yolofsky and Enrique Prado deserve thanks for their public support and efforts. I am also grateful to Kim and Oliver Pimley and Jackson Graham for their continuous dedication as supporters and kravists, along with Art Co and Victor Velez for their support and for explaining the nuances of Philippine-edged weapons tactics. The Tenenbaums and Goldbergs remain pillars of my life and mishpachat. I'd like to give special thanks to the family of James Gandolfini. I thank John Mayer for his support. I also extend my thanks to Justin Kingson and the late Bill Kingson. Steven Feldstein is an exceptional man and as tough and determined as they come. I thank him for his support. I am also extremely grateful to Gary Solomon, Esq., for his intellectual property insights and support. Sorat Tungkasari merits a special thanks as a great friend and advocate. I also thank Josh Caputo for his exceptional hand-to-hand combat insights and support.

A special thanks on both a personal and professional level to all of our friends and supporters in the law enforcement community, including Trooper Joe Drew; Sergeant Mike Delahanty; Captain (Ret.) Miller; Sergeant (Ret.) McComb; Sergeant (Ret.) Klem; Sergeant Oehlmann; Sergeant Rayhon; Captain (Ret.) Maimone; Major Ponenti; Lieutenant DeMaise; Lieutenant Wolf; Lieutenant Cowan; Sergeant Boland; Lieutenant Capriglione; Lieutenant Peins; Officer Vaval; Captain Crowe; Captain (Ret.) Savalli; Officer Vacirca; Associate Director Harrison; Chief Lazzarotti; Director Paglione; Investigators Smith and Gioscio; Officer Starky; Officer Tucker; Officer Hanafee; Lieutenant Colon; Sergeant Hayden; Officer Johnson; Special Agent-in-Charge Hammond; Special agents Bercume Schroeder, Belle, Love, Clark, Nowazcek, and Crowe; Colonel Corey Britcher; Officer Albert Carson II; Trooper Gary W.; Sergeant Al Lopez; Lieutenant Rabinovitz; Chief Sutter; Lieutenant Currier and the entire Princeton Police Department, along with the many other law enforcement professionals with whom we have the honor of working.

I thank the following U.S. Marine Corps personnel: Lieutenant Colonel (Ret.) Joseph Shusko; Gunnery Sergeant Gokey; Master Gunnery Sergeant (Ret.) Urso; Sergeants Ladler, Parker, and Allen; Lieutenant Colonel "Tonto" Ardese; Staff Sergeant Jensen; Corporal Lackland; Staff Sergeant Kropelwicki; Sergeant Ben Perkins of the Royal Marines, along with Major Haigh of the U.S. Air Force; First Sergeant Johnson; Major (Ret.) Hoggs; Captain Ansur; and Technical Sergeant Eric Testerman for their support. Thanks also to all of our fighting men and women of the U.S. military and the Israel Defense Forces for safeguarding our freedom. Security expert Steven Hartov, one of my favorite authors and good friends, deserves much gratitude for his personal and professional support. I am grateful to Drs. Steven Gecha, Stephen Hunt, Bruce Rose, and PTs Lindsey Balint and Jeff Manheimer, who continue to hold me together. Thanks to Jerry Palmieri for his conditioning advice, along with George Samuelson and "Doc" Mark Cheng. I am grateful to the late Master Lowell Slaven for his exceptional support and professional insights. Lowell was truly a paragon of martial arts teaching and leadership. He was a mentor to me and countless others, demonstrating a rare breed of unfettered integrity, selflessness, backing, and backbone. He is dearly missed.

I am indebted to all my krav maga friends, supporters, network, and fellow instructors Frank Colluci, Jeff Gorman, Mike Delahanty, David Ordini, Alec Goenner, Corey Davis, Alex Feinberg, David Gollin, George Foster, Jason Bleitstein, Joe Tucker, Chris Morrison, Al Ackerman, Joe Drew, Jose Anaya, Kelly Arlinghaus, Mimi Rowland, Bill Dwyer, Bevin Jones, Kevin Scorzarro, Mark and Joey Miller, John Papp, Mike McElvin, Paul Karleen, David Ravencroft, and Ronnie James Hughes, along with all those instructors in the pipeline. Instructor David Rahn made the pivotal suggestion that made this book come alive. I am in Paul Karleen's debt for his editing insights and teaching support. I am grateful to all our students both at our Israeli and United States krav maga training centers (www.israelikrav.com).

Select immediate and extended family members have always been a buttress and a wellspring of support—especially my wife, Claire, for some subtle editing; my mother, Anne; my stepfather, Ed; my uncle Harry; along with my father, Alfred—for the growth of krav maga training and redoubt of support for our exacting expansion. I trust Benjamin and Leo will be the next generation of kravists following krav maga founder Imi Lichtenfeld's credo of emphasizing good citizenship and a humble "sense of self-worth."

PREFACE

THE MATERIAL OFFERED IN THIS BOOK IS a compact, essential overview of krav maga's core techniques for defending against and defeating what I consider to be the twelve most common unarmed street attacks:

1. Pushes

2. Arm and shirt grabs

3. Hook or haymaker punches

4. Straight punches

5. Kick or knee attacks to the groin

6. Headbutts

7. Chokes and headlocks

8. Takedowns

9. Bear hugs

10. When on your back

11. Mounts

12. Guards and stomps

Also included is a brief overview of specific subtopics and tactics to avoid violence:

1. An introduction to violence and the krav maga mind-set

2. Preconflict indicators

3. Conflict avoidance

4. **Conflict de-escalation**

5. **Conflict escape and evasion**

6. **The mind and body's reactions when confronted with physical violence**

While entire chapters or even books could be devoted to each of these subtopics, in the interest of providing a concise approach, I have attempted to introduce some of the most significant discussion and learning points and to make these topics accessible to all levels of practitioners. I have purposefully repeated certain strategic and tactical precepts, as the importance of these krav maga tenets cannot be overemphasized.

Krav maga, the Israeli self-defense system, was created by the late Imi Lichtenfeld. Grandmaster Haim Gidon, the current president of the IKMA (Israeli Krav Maga Association), continually strives to develop, enhance, and improve the krav maga system on a daily basis. I hope this book serves as a solid introduction for those interested in learning more about krav maga. It also is designed to complement my previous two books, *Krav Maga: An Essential Guide* and *Advanced Krav Maga* along with DVD Volume IV *Mastering Krav Maga: Defending the 12 Most Common Unarmed Attacks*. In addition, I hope this information provides an instructive review for seasoned krav maga practitioners and martial artists alike, as it touches on several key core-technique subtleties. Representative of our teaching aims, I quote the late, great Gracie Jiu-Jitsu grandmaster Helio Gracie, "To teach those who don't know, to remind those who do know, to correct those who think they know." For those who convert this material and represent it as their own without attribution, you know who you are and we know who you are.

BECAUSE NOT ALL KRAV MAGA IS THE SAME™ . . .

INTRODUCTION

THE ISRAELI KRAV MAGA ADVANTAGE

RESPONSIBLE PEOPLE PURSUE ISRAELI KRAV MAGA TRAINING TO SHIELD THEM-

SELVES FROM VIOLENCE, NOT TO ORCHESTRATE VIOLENCE. THE KRAVIST TRAINS

AND PREPARES HIMSELF TO FACE DOWN THE UNFORTUNATE, UGLY SPECTER OF

VIOLENCE. KRAV MAGA TRAINING, BY BOTH NECESSITY AND RESULTANT DESIGN, focuses on the realistic and brutal nature of a physical assault. This self-defense and fighting system is designed to thwart and neutralize any type of threat or attack. The key survival ingredient is your mind-set. Those who train physically and mentally to preempt and, if necessary, thwart violence with overwhelming counterviolence will respond differently from people who do not condition themselves.

You, the kravist, when threatened or attacked, must unleash a torrent of overwhelming counterviolence. (This assumes there is no peaceful option and the circumstances are legally justified.) Krav maga's goal is to neutralize an attacker quickly and decisively. If you must defend yourself, krav maga enables you to effectively stun, incapacitate, and, if necessary, control your attacker. Your honed, instinctive reaction will turn the tables on your attacker(s) immediately. Krav maga tactics are designed as defensive-capability multipliers. A few mastered krav maga techniques are highly effective in most situations. When properly learned and practiced, these tactics will become first nature.

CONFLICT AVOIDANCE

Nonviolent conflict avoidance is always your best solution. The following is the most important lesson krav maga can teach you: Do not to be taken by surprise or caught in the "-5." (The "-5" is when one is unprepared to fight for one's life.) Becoming an accomplished observer helps you resolve a situation before it fully evolves or gets out of hand. By constantly surveying your locale and its dynamics, you will notice at all times who and what surrounds you.

Walking away from a confrontation is a test of mental discipline and moral fiber. For example, if a situation involves someone taunting you, attempting to embarrass you, or assert social hierarchy, take the sensible action and walk away. Should you (correctly) walk away, be sure to disengage with a heightened sense of potential confrontation awareness. Until you are safe, continue to maintain both a mental and physical preparedness to spring into action. Extricating yourself from a potentially violent situation is both wise and pragmatic for myriad reasons, including avoiding potential injury to you and your family and avoiding criminal and civil liability proceedings.

Use common sense, basic precautions, and a confident demeanor to minimize your chances of being targeted and assaulted. Notwithstanding these preventive measures, accept the possibility of violence targeting you. There are several types of violence, including social, criminal, sociopathic, and professional. Statistically, you are most likely to face the first or second categories, social or criminal, respectively. Terrorism usually falls into a blend of the latter two categories. While you need not live in fear, denial is the most common obstacle to taking appropriate action. This is why you must be prepared, if you must face down a violent situation. Sharpen your mental and physical skills so you can implement them without thinking.

INSTINCTIVE, AGGRESSIVE REACTION IS REQUIRED

When in danger, your brain and body respond reflexively. Therefore, your self-defense reaction must be both instantaneously reflexive and instinctive. If you are in a fight and an attacker makes an unanticipated or unrecognized action, the brain cannot find a practiced response, resulting in decision paralysis. By training to respond, you will call upon your instincts and reflexes when attacked. With proper training, you will learn to conquer your fear and to control the energy and power from your body's fight-or-flight response. Realistic training is designed to eliminate the third human reaction, a freeze response. You will learn not to freeze under pressure. While it is unusual to be in a situation where you must fight for your life, it does happen. You must be prepared.

Krav maga harnesses your natural abilities for you to (re)act optimally with little cognitive interference. With practice, you will be able to explode into action. Your attacker will literally not know what hit him—repeatedly. Only serious, hard, and appropriate training can trigger this fighting response. If push comes to shove, literally and figuratively, krav maga is designed to handle any type or number of assaults. For a kravist, there are no set solutions for ending a fight. A kravist may have different physical strengths and capabilities. He may have a strong kick or hand-strike capabilities; or strong infighting; or throwing skills; or takedowns, etc. This book will provide you some of the simplest and most effective defensive and counterattack measures.

There are no rules in street defense. This essential tenet distinguishes self-defense from sport fighting. In a scripted sport fight the following nonexclusive tactics are generally banned: eye gouge; throat strikes; headbutting; biting; hair-pulling; clawing, pinching, or twisting of the flesh; striking the spine and the back of the head; striking with the tip of the elbow; small-joint manipulation; kidney and liver strikes, clavicle strikes; kneeing or kicking the head of an attacker on the ground; and slamming an attacker to the ground on the attacker's head. These are exactly the combined core tactics krav maga emphasizes.

If you must fight, identify the opportune moment to attack the attacker with a continuous overwhelming counterattack using retzev or "continuous combat motion." Combined with simultaneous defense and attack or near-simultaneous defense and attack, retzev is a seamless, decisive, and overpowering counterattack forming the backbone of the Israeli fighting system. Retzev may be understood as using combined upper- and lower-body combatives, locks, chokes, throws, takedowns, and weapons interchangeably and without pause.

Exert maximum speed and aggression. Your goal is not to definitively win a fight, but, rather, to escape. Never forget that the level of force you use to defend yourself should be commensurate with the threat. Once the threat is no more, you must cease counteroffensive actions. The krav maga system is designed to conform to you. You do not need to conform to the system or adopt any rigid, set solutions. To be sure, there are preferred counterattack methods using retzev to prevail, but you must react instinctively to the best of your ability.

TRAINING

With proper intense training, you will learn effective physical tactics, while mentally adjusting to a harsh, violent reality. When training, practice the select krav maga methods in the upcoming chapters under extreme simulated pressure. Train in the most realistic setting possible to develop the mental preparedness you need to react in life-threatening situations. As you repeat techniques and situations at real speed (with safety in mind), you'll develop your fighting prowess. To reemphasize, your krav maga techniques will become your automatic reflex whenever you find yourself in danger.

To adopt and streamline the krav maga method, personalize the techniques and make them your own. Choose the ballistic strikes and other combatives with which you feel most comfortable and that give you the greatest confidence. Put just as much emphasis on mental training as you do the physical through visualization and scenario planning. You can also use your mind to train your body to automatically and instinctively react to danger. Visualization and scenario planning can boost your confidence, reduce fear, improve your fighting technique, and help you cope with unanticipated hostile situations, because you will have envisioned them beforehand.

By visualizing a new experience, you deposit a new conditioned response into your memory bank. You perform routine tasks such as covering your mouth when you sneeze, because these tasks are just that, routine. They become routine by repetition. By visualizing possible situations and your reactions to them over and over again, your brain immediately recalls your reaction whenever you physically find yourself in such a situation, and you react accordingly.

Your brain does not distinguish between the actual tasks you physically perform and the ones you imagine or visualize. If you're unsure about this, think about watching an unexpected violent real-life encounter on the Internet and how you may cringe or blink in disbelief. Similarly, have you ever felt your heart beating or palms sweating while watching a realistic suspense thriller? Notably, athletes are thoroughly versed in the powers of visualization and have used it with great success.

EMPHASIS ON A FEW CORE TACTICS

Krav maga emphasizes learning a few elementary core tactics that can be performed instinctively and adapted to myriad situations. If necessary, you will know how to maim an attacker by striking vital points and organs or applying choking or breaking pressure to an attacker's joints. The goal is to embed your subconscious with the proverbial "(I have) been there, done that (through a training scenario)." Therefore, your autonomic response is, indeed, "I've been there, done that."

Optimally, the potential confrontation is over before it can begin. You have neutralized the threat at its inception. Most important, you should have confidence in your krav maga training, because all techniques are battle-tested and field-proven. Do not, however, mistake your training for a real attack. In an actual attack you'll experience an adrenaline surge and a likely decrease in your fine motor skills, your heart rate will skyrocket, your hearing will diminish ("auditory exclusion"), and your vision will narrow (often known as "tunnel vision"). Notably, most people who have survived violent confrontations had the mental commitment to prevail. They do not often attribute their survival to a specific technique.

LEGAL CONSIDERATIONS

However and whenever krav maga self-defense might be used, it must be legally justified, incorporating the appropriate level of counterforce. For non-deadly force, the law generally recognizes that a person may use such force as reasonably necessary to thwart the imminent use of force against that person, short of deadly force. Note that you may step into the shoes of a third party to intervene, using and meeting a specific state's standard.

The law in most countries evaluates a person's response according to an objective "reasonable person standard." For self-defense, the operative language becomes "reasonable force." In other words, what would the reasonable person do, or how would an objective, reasonable person react, under the totality of the circumstances?

Only fear of imminent bodily harm provides justification to use force. Objective reasonable force is best viewed on a sliding scale. The level of force employed is often dependent on an assailant's capability, opportunity, and intent. You can measure an attacker's capability in several ways. A weapon, large physical size, or displayed martial prowess such as a fighting stance, generally indicates the assailant's measure of capability.

American law, for example, generally recognizes a "disparity of force," when an attacker possesses recognizable physical advantages or prowess such as significant height, strength, and weight advantages, or displayed trained fighting skills, when adjudicating liability and criminal charges. In addition, environment might also influence more force, as, for example, in struggling next to a busy highway where you could be flung into onrushing traffic.

Force, especially lethal force, is generally never justifiable to protect property. For example, if someone keys your car, spits at you, or knocks over your mailbox, you may not resort to force to settle the score. To use physical force to defend yourself, you must have a reasonable fear of harm. Only when you fear for your own life or that of another should you use lethal force.

For deadly force, state laws generally recognize that a person may use such force as reasonable to prevent serious bodily injury (mayhem) or death. If you must resort to violence to protect yourself, you must be able to explain to a jury why and how you chose your actions and that there were no reasonable alternatives. This is counterbalanced against the understanding that any given physical confrontation has the potential to kill you.

Developed as a military fighting discipline, krav maga employs lethal force tech-

ISRAELI KRAV MAGA'S TACTICAL TEN COMMANDMENTS

1. Israeli krav maga works against any attacker; the key is your mind-set. Never accept defeat or surrender. If you can breathe, you can fight. Do what you must to prevail.

2. Assess your surroundings. Common sense, basic precautions, and a confident demeanor minimize your chances of being attacked.

3. Nonviolent conflict resolution is always your best solution. De-escalate and disengage when possible.

4. A few mastered techniques go a long way and are highly effective in most situations.

5. The essence of krav maga is to neutralize an attacker quickly; there are no rules.

6. A strategy to end your attacker's fighting ability is paramount when using simultaneous defense and attack. Fight positioning by moving off the line of attack determines your tactical advantage.

7. Footwork and body positioning, whether standing or prone, allow you to simultaneously defend and attack allowing for seamless combative transitions, essential to perform retzev or "continuous combat motion."

8. Optimally, a kravist will move quickly to a superior and dominant position, the "dead side" to finish the fight. You dictate the fight using retzev combatives.

9. Dead-side strategy revolves around your capabilities and preferred tactics involving long, medium, and short combatives combined with evasive maneuvers. This positioning becomes even more important when facing multiple attackers.

10. Retzev is seamlessly using all parts of your body for an overwhelming, decisive counterattack. Combined with simultaneous defense and attack, retzev is the backbone of the Israeli fighting system.

niques. When faced with a deadly force encounter, you may, in turn, need to employ lethal counterforce. Forging an awareness of your own personal weapons (hands, forearms, elbows, knees shins, feet, and head) and an attacker's vulnerabilities is essential to fight strategy and tactics, especially when he is armed and you are not. The human body is amazingly resilient, even when subjected to tremendous physical abuse. Pain may stop some attackers, but other individuals have enormous pain thresholds, especially if they are taking narcotics.

To assess the necessity of counterviolence, you must instantly gauge several factors, including your opportunity to retreat. Retreat can be problematic, if you are with another party such as a child or an elderly companion. Importantly, reacting from surprise allows the use of more force because you do not have time to rationally or reasonably analyze the situation. The moment you are deemed safe, any additional defensive actions may, in fact, become offensive actions. If you continue to injure an assailant who is no longer a threat, you could face civil and criminal charges, especially if you deliberately turn an assailant's weapon on him.

You'll need to articulate that you had no choice when faced with a threat who had the:

- **Intent (stated or evident goal of harming you)**
- **Capability (has the prowess or tools to harm you)**
- **Opportunity (proximity)**

Notably, intent often involves the wielding of a weapon and verbal threats to life and limb. If any of the above three criteria is absent or becomes absent or you could avoid the threat, you are no longer acting in self-defense.

Once legal proceedings begin, whatever measures you took to defend yourself will most certainly be painted in different lights by an accuser/opposing counsel and your counsel in your legal defense. Your legal justification for your self-defense actions may center on the following points:

- **How well can you articulate the reasons for your actions?**
- **Was your counterviolence warranted (using the reasonableness standard) to contend with the immediacy of the assault?**

Even if you prevail in criminal court, you are likely to face civil charges, including aggravated assault, and might have to face compensating the injured party for lost earnings, medical bills, pain, and suffering, along with the prospective of a jury awarding punitive damages to teach you a lesson. It cannot be emphasized enough, when defending yourself, that you are only entitled to use the amount of force that is commensurate with the threat. As tempting as it might be to severely hurt or kill your assailant, you must make a deliberate conscious decision when to cease your counterattack. If you use counterviolence, you must believe the stakes are real and the aggressor is playing for keeps.

Throughout this book, the following terms will appear frequently. Once you understand the language of krav maga, you will better understand the method.

COMBATIVE: Any manner of strike, takedown, throw, joint lock, choke, or other offensive fighting movement.

"-5": A description created by Sergeant Major (Ret.) Nir Maman for when you are initially unprepared to fight for your life. You are ambushed.

RETZEV: A Hebrew word that means "continuous motion" in combat. Retzev, the backbone of modern Israeli krav maga, teaches you to move your body instinctively in combat motion without thinking about your next move. When in a dangerous situation, you will automatically call upon your physical and mental training to launch a seamless overwhelming counterattack using integrated combatives combined with evasive action. Retzev is quick and decisive movement merging all aspects of your krav maga training. Defensive movements transition automatically into offensive movements to neutralize the attack—affording your attacker little time to react.

LEFT OUTLET STANCE: Blades your body by turning your feet approximately 30 degrees to your right, with your left arm and left leg forward. (You can also turn 30 degrees to your right to come into a right regular outlet stance, so that your right leg and arm are forward.) You are resting on the balls of both of your feet with your rear foot in a comfortable and balanced position. Your feet should be parallel, with about 55% of your weight distributed over your front leg. Your arms are positioned in front of your face and bent slightly forward at approximately a 60-degree angle between your forearms and your upper arms. From this stance, you will move forward, laterally, and backward, moving your feet in concert.

TAI SABAKI: A Japanese term relating to "whole body movement" or tactical repositioning. Tai sabaki footwork usually involves a semicircular movement or up to a 180-degree step with one foot to move the body. It can be used to avoid an attack or to take an attacker down using a wristlock, positioning the defender in an advantageous position.

LIVE SIDE: When you are facing the front of your attacker and your attacker can both see you and use all four arms and legs against you, you are facing the attacker's live side.

DEAD SIDE: Your attacker's dead side, in contrast to the attacker's live side, places you behind the attacker's near shoulder or facing the attacker's back. You are in an advantageous position to counterattack and control the attacker, because it is difficult for the attacker to use his far arm and leg to attack you. You should always move to the dead side when possible. This also places the attacker between you and any additional third-party threat.

SAME SIDE: Your same-side arm or leg faces your attacker when you are positioned opposite one another. For example, if you are directly facing your attacker and your right side is opposite your attacker's left side, your same-side arm is your right arm (opposite the attacker's left arm).

NEAR SIDE: Your limb closest to the attacker.

OUTSIDE DEFENSE: An outside defense counters an outside attack, that is, an attack directed at you from the outside of your body to the inside. A slap to the face or hook punch are examples of outside attacks.

INSIDE DEFENSE: An inside defense defends against an inside or straight attack. This type of attack involves a thrusting motion such as jabbing your finger into someone's eye or punching someone in the nose.

GUNT: A deflection or absorption of an incoming strike by bending your elbow to touch your bicep to your forearm. The angle of deflection depends on the strike. For example, to defend against a hook punch or roundhouse kick to the head, you will position the elbow to cover your head with the back of your arm parallel to the ground, with the elbow tip facing slightly outward. The gunt may also be used to defend against knee attacks by jamming the attacker's knee with the tip of the elbow.

GLICHA: A sliding movement on the balls of your feet to carry your entire body weight forward and through a combative strike to maximize its impact.

OFF ANGLE: An attack angle that is not face-to-face.

STEPPING OFF THE LINE: Using footwork and body movement to take evasive action against a linear attack such as a straight punch or kick. Such movement is also referred to as breaking the angle of attack.

TRAPPING: Occurs when you pin or grab the attacker's arms with one arm, leaving you with a free arm to continue combatives.

MOUNT: A formidable control fighting and position where you are straddling your attacker with the attacker's back to the ground and your heels are hooked underneath the attacker's rib cage.

REAR MOUNT: The most advantageous control position on the ground, where you are behind and straddling your attacker (who may be faceup or facedown) with your legs wrapped—not crossed—around the attacker's midsection.

TIME IN MOTION: The time it takes a combative to reach a target and what the human target's physical response to a landed combative is likely to be. This includes an attacker's physical response to your counterattack(s).

KINESIC INDICATORS: The recognition and interpretation of nonverbal body movement, including facial expressions and gestures.

KRAVIST: A term I coined in *Krav Maga: An Essential Guide to the Renowned Method—for Fitness and Self-Defense* to describe a smart and prepared krav maga fighter.

ONE

VIOLENCE, SELF-DEFENSE, EFFECTS, AND CONSEQUENCES

STREET VIOLENCE IS VOLATILE, UNPREDICTABLE, AND OFTEN UNANNOUNCED

(THOUGH THERE MAY BE PREVIOLENCE INDICATORS A VICTIM DID NOT RECOG-

NIZE). THERE ARE NO CERTAINTIES REGARDING THE OUTCOME OF A POTENTIAL

LIFE-AND-DEATH STRUGGLE. AN ATTACKER WILL LIKELY SEEK EVERY ADVANTAGE.

FOUR GENERAL TYPES OF VIOLENCE

There are four general reasons for common types of violence:

1. **APPREHENSION**: You represent some sort of threat to another person (or animal).
   - **NONVIOLENT SOLUTION**: De-escalate using a nonthreatening manner, including open palms and a slow, calm, conciliatory approach and voice. Note: One of the more common provocations can be invading someone's personal space.

2. **EGO-DRIVEN**: Someone wishes to exert social dominance or has perceived an affront from you creating an excuse to pull the violence trigger.
   - **NONVIOLENT SOLUTION**: De-escalate by using a nonthreatening manner, including open palms, a slow, calm approach, along with a conciliatory voice, and, within reason, capitulating to the aggressor's demands or will.

3. **RAGE OR EMOTIONALLY DISTURBED**: You become the target because the attacker is independently set off by something real or perceived that you did or you just happen to be in the attacker's sights.
   - **NONVIOLENT SOLUTION**: Ignore the attacker. If you cannot avoid the attacker, establish a firm boundary clearly delineating that you will not be a victim. Your body language unequivocally establishes that you will meet any force with overwhelming countervailing force. Be aware that there are mentally anguished people spoiling for a fight no matter what the odds of success. There is no chance of reasoning or de-escalation. The only solution is avoidance or incapacitating these types of aggressors.

4. **CRIMINAL**: You have something the attacker wants.
   - **NONVIOLENT SOLUTION**: Give the attacker what the attacker wants "within reason." Within reason must include not violating your body or going to a potential secondary crime scene. Your only other solution may be to immediately incapacitate the criminal aggressor.

First and foremost, he will try to use the element of surprise. You may find yourself in a "-5" position or initially unprepared to fight for your life.

Concerted, determined violence seldom lasts more than a few seconds. Adopting a simple survival mind-set is inadequate. You must believe you will physically win without sustaining any permanent physical damage. Regardless of an attacker's size, strength, training, or physical ability, you will prevail by delivering debilitating, overwhelming counterviolence. Essential to survival is your mental and psychological tenacity. Mental training envisions not just defending oneself (after all other precautions and de-escalation measures have failed), but, when necessary, also damaging another human or, in rare cases, an animal.

Three highly recommended books to further explore the different strata, forms, and evolutions of violence are Rory Miller's *Meditations on Violence, Facing Violence,* and *ConCom: Conflict Communications.* You can often recognize verbal, behavioral, and physical manifestations indicating that violence is imminent. Recognized or not, there will be some indicator prior to an attack.

Obviously, social violence is more prevalent when people are under the influence of alcohol or drugs or when young men congregate. Importantly, young males often feel they have much to prove and do not fully understand violence's ramifications: physical, psychological, and legal. Introducing a weapon changes the stakes and indicates a possible willingness to maim or kill. When verbal reasoning ceases, if krav maga is your solution, there must be no other available choice.

SOCIAL VIOLENCE

Humans have subconscious rules governing social violence. The contest of teaching someone a lesson by asserting social dominance by either intimidation or physical force usually does not involve grave injuries or murderous intent. Yet, you should never underestimate the capability, determination, or cunning of an attacker. Generally, someone will only attack if the person thinks he can physically win. A criminal or sociopath may have little formal fight or martial arts training; however, the attacker compensates for this with a deeply embedded, unflappable resolve to injure you.

When facing the specter of social violence, if no body contact is made with you, as glib as it may sound, if there is "no harm, (then there is) no foul." Despite any indignation or effrontery you may experience, walk away from the situation. Perhaps, by adopting the mind-set that it was the aggressor's lucky day or that you would have "beat him down," you can more easily swallow your ego and disengage. The flip side is that you do not know what the aggressor's capabilities and intent are. So, in either case, use common sense, not inflamed emotions, to carry the day and walk away. Founder Imi Lichtenfeld emphasized, "The most necessary thing is to educate you—and that is the hardest thing—to be humble. You must be so humble that you don't want to show him that you're better than him. That is one of the most necessary things for pupils. If a pupil tells me, 'I fought him and beat him,' it's no good."[1]

Scientists have noted that evolution wired our brains to generally avoid killing (a hardwired safety mechanism) when testing social dominance. With animals and humans alike, hierarchical conflict is rarely lethal, but males, in particular, often have difficulty backing down from status conflict. The reality is that some people will tolerate effrontery and abuse while others will not. Those who are intolerant of challenges may have a shorter or longer fuse, but eventually this fuse will ignite.

Amateur social violence occurs, for example, when Aggressor #1 (A1) is not entirely committed to injuring Aggressor #2 (A2). A1 hopes one combative will likely hurt or subdue, but, importantly, not truly injure A2 to deter him from continuing. In summary, the goal of amateur violence is to "put a hurt" on someone, but not to truly injure the attacker. The takeaway is that you should recognize impending social violence and not let it control or dictate your future.

CRIMINAL VIOLENCE

When confronting possible criminal violence, it is axiomatic that your life and well-being are not worth trading for any possessions. A criminal uses violence as a physical tool to acquire valuables. If someone is threatening you, especially with a weapon or if you are clearly outnumbered, comply with the criminal's demands—if you can. If you cannot comply with the aggressor's demands, and reasoning with the aggressor has failed and there is no escape, take the fight to your assailant to neutralize him. As noted, maintaining an overall strategy to end your attacker's ability to harm you is paramount.

While criminal or sociopathic violence is less likely, these categories must be dealt with differently than social violence. There is no opt-out option. (Remember, there is an opt-out option when confronting social violence.) Generally, under these circumstances, an aggressor cannot be reasoned with or "talked down." There is no disengagement strategy available to you—other than to use superior counterviolence. If your actions require a forceful and debilitating counterviolent response, krav maga provides it.

---

1. Julia M. Klein, "Don't Get Hurt," *Philadelphia Inquirer*, April 9, 1984.

Raw Criminal Violence

Raw criminal violence is more prevalent in isolated places, which provides privacy for predators. Criminology studies underscore that criminals usually rely more on intent rather than a specific (trained) method of violence. Criminals do not operate using the same set of accepted social beliefs as their victims, who respect the social contract and obey the law.

Professional military and law enforcement personnel use overwhelming violence of action and a preponderance of firepower. Criminals try to do the same. The predatory assault mind-set is ruthless. Some attackers view their targets as humans, while other sociopath attackers can "dehumanize" or make someone an outsider, thereby denying any social contract. "Dehumanizing" can pave the way for violence by distinguishing or rationalizing another person's humanity away. The attacker need not necessarily be physically skilled. If he succeeds in stunning the victim, he can compound the damage, requiring little ability other than targeting the victim's vulnerable anatomy.

Emotionally Disturbed Violence

When dealing with an aggressor with an altered mind, rational rules of human behavior do not apply. One solution when dealing with a mentally impaired aggressive individual is to avoid direct eye contact while listening passively and disarmingly. Nevertheless, expect the unexpected and, accordingly, be prepared physically. A sociopath views asocial criminal violence as a useful tool. Pleading with a sociopath usually will not succeed. To counter asocial criminal violence where there may be no quarter given to you, you must break down the attacker's body.

Note: Rape can fall into both criminal and sociopathic categories.

Not coincidentally, krav maga's core method of using optimized counterviolence— retzev—may be compared to the type of professional or military assault discussed above. Accordingly, under the strict legal underpinnings of self-defense, if attacked, the kravist must become the more violently capable person, wielding greater counterforce to defeat the threat. Targeted counterviolence designed to injure an attacker leads to a conclusive result: the scale of physical power tilts in the kravist's favor.

Social Violence (Unspoken Rules) vs. Raw Violence (No Rules)	
Social Violence ■ vestige of rules (mayhem/death is not the preferred outcome)	Raw Violence ■ no rules (resulting in mayhem/death)

TACTICAL AND STRATEGIC THINKING FOR MEN AND WOMEN ALIKE

Both men and women alike should try to achieve a paradoxical balance between: (1) living without fear and (2) paranoia. Constant vigilance drains energy and cannot be maintained. Therefore, your radar has to adapt to ping what generally seems to be out of the ordinary. Awareness provides you time to recognize threats and to act, rather than react. Awareness of what is behind you could be more important than what is in front of you. Obviously, the best way to catch someone by surprise is from the rear. First impressions or gut feelings are usually correct. Trust your intuition; don't dismiss it. If you recognize that something is amiss, beware. Your intuition is undergirded by your experience and accumulated knowledge. A highly recommended book focusing on the vital use of one's intuition is Gavin de Becker's *The Gift of Fear*.

When there is no other choice, you may be compelled to maim, cripple, and even use lethal force against an attacker—provided the respective circumstances are legally justifiable. Breaking bones and disabling ligaments, destroying an eyeball, etc., are optimized both tactically and strategically to end the attack. In the basest, animalistic sense, the kravist, when faced with a life-threatening situation, understands how to inflict terrible, debilitating wounds against an adversary. Once again, there is no pity or humanity in a visceral self-defense situation, provided the counterforce is legally justifiable. In general terms, the party who significantly damages the other party first usually prevails, provided he presses the counterattack home to neutralize the threat.

Ignoring unsolicited entreaties will serve you well. You need not be civil if your instincts tell you to behave otherwise. Be sure to understand the difference between an aggressive and assertive response when confronting a possible threat. Assertiveness is essential and one of the most effective strategies to preventing assault. If you lack assertiveness, you can develop this deterrence capability by modifying your body posture.

Violence against women often involves men who seek status by targeting women to assert dominance. Many female victims know their attackers. Sexual predators and other attackers often approach their victims with innocuous behavior such as friendly conversation. Sometimes, a potential assailant will put his hand on a woman to gauge her initial reaction. If she is not assertive in warning him off, he may have found a potential victim in his mind. If she opposes him either verbally or physically or both, he has found someone who will actively resist, and, therefore, is likely a less successful target.

Generally, the male attacker believes he can assault a woman and come away unscathed physically. (This is true of most attackers regardless of the attacker or victim's respective genders.) According to Professor James Giannini of Ohio State University, female rape victims are often less attuned to interpreting nonverbal facial cues of an assailant.[1] This situational awareness shortcoming may make them miss the all-important warning signs of aggressive criminal intent. The same research suggests that rapists are more capable than average to interpret facial cues in women who will not resist.[2] Predatory men understand that social conditioning for women teaches placating or submission, as women are frequently conditioned to interact with men verbally rather than offer physical resistance.

Violence against women often involves close proximity or "infighting," especially during a sexual assault. It is often ingrained that resistance will trigger a more severe onslaught. Yet, according to the National Institute of Justice, "Most self-protective actions significantly reduce the risk that a rape will be completed. In particular, certain actions reduce the risk of rape more than 80 percent compared to nonresistance. The most effective actions, according to victims, are attacking or struggling against their attacker, running away, and verbally warning the attacker."[3] Please note that this book focuses on street-oriented violence rather then domestic violence. Hence, this important topic is not examined here.

Holding your head high, presenting a comfortable and confident demeanor, maintaining eye contact, clutching a weapon of opportunity, and moving with a purpose will help de-victimize you. Studies show that criminals often target people who do not walk with confidence, pay attention, or have coordinated gait. These people appeared to the criminal to be easy targets who are not likely to fight back.

1. www.psychologytoday.com/articles/200812/marked-mayhem.

2. www.psychologytoday.com/articles/200812/marked-mayhem.

3. www.nij.gov/topics/crime/rape-sexual-violence/campus/pages/decrease-risk.aspx.

AWARENESS METHODS

One of the most effective tactics krav maga teaches you is not to be taken by surprise in the first place. The Israeli krav maga curriculum places heavy emphasis on the ability to recognize, avoid, and/or preempt physical conflicts. Developing recognition of previolence indicators along with impending attacks is instrumental to krav maga. The obvious and best solution is to remove yourself from the situation before an impending attack can take place. Situational awareness regarding whom to keenly observe is all-important, and common sense should prevail. Recognize who or what might constitute a danger or threat.

Generally, human behavior is overwhelmingly predictable. Therefore, you must identify what are normal human behavior patterns and what are anomalous behavior displays. For example, someone, constantly looking over his shoulder should merit enhanced scrutiny. Or, as another example, an unknown person trying to subtly get close to you warrants immediate attention. Further, you need to distinguish what is crucial information versus what is noncrucial.

Subtle cues, "tells," or "precipitators" observed in a potential assailant's behavior, especially when such indicators are assessed collectively, provide an early warning indicator. In other words, recognizing someone's preparation to perpetrate an assault, such as the attacker's (un)conscious body language (including autonomic nervous system reactions), proximity and overall behavior pattern, produces clues you can discern. Body markings, such as tattoos, can also suggest someone's background, affiliation, values, attitude, and behavioral proclivities. Understanding these clues allows you to become proactive or what the U.S. Marines describe as having a "bias for action" leading to, if necessary, krav maga "violence of action."

Being proactive overcomes victimization. If you perceive a potential threat, take preemptive action and extricate yourself. Clearly, the best defense against any attack is avoiding or removing yourself from the precarious situation. Once again, common sense should succeed. If an environment suggests an overall negative feeling or "vibe," heed your internal warning and take appropriate safety measures. Only environmental and situational awareness, along with recognition training, can help you do that.

In an unfamiliar environment, scan for threats, paying particular attention to potential adversaries' proximity and hand movements. Make use of your peripheral vision and constantly assess your surroundings. For example, if a man is in a bathroom using a urinal, he should use the chrome flushing mechanism as a modified mirror to scan behind him or keep his head tilted to look over his shoulder.

As previously noted, situational awareness is a compromise between being carefree and paranoid. Most people have this innate capability. As a general example, take a pedestrian crosswalk across a road: as you prepare to cross the street, the car approaching slows down, but you still watch for it to come to a complete stop. You assume the car will do so, but do not bind your fate entirely to your presumption.

Humans usually can only successfully perform one task or function at a time. With your innate danger-detection capability in mind, if someone is going through the motions of some act but displays an odd interest in you, obviously, your defenses correctly go on high alert. Be sure to trust this well-placed intuition. Simply put, if someone acts nervous, secretive, or unnatural and the person is within attack range of you, beware; take the appropriate defensive precautions.

Self-defense may be thought of as recovering from being caught unaware (the "-5") and using (superior) counterviolence in the same way a criminal or sociopath intends to use his assault on you. Many people are wholly unprepared to face down violence even when they see it coming. These victims of violence do not understand indicators or they do not recognize the foreshadowing "tells."

Awareness or recognition of an impending attack/threat obviously affords the greatest reaction time for the following seriatim solutions: (a) avoidance, (b) de-escalation, (c) escape, and (d) counterviolence. Always trust your instincts and intuition, including things you saw, heard, felt or smelled—all your senses—the things your subconscious brain intakes and processes faster than your conscious mind can keep up. Importantly, only a minimal amount of threatening behavioral information is enough for you to put your defenses on high alert.

For self-defense, the aphorism "forewarned is forearmed" is particularly salient. In an unknown environment, keep your head subtly swiveling by shifting your eye movements, using your peripheral vision, and panning for potential threats. Constantly survey your surroundings. Keep in mind that when you are mentally focused or consumed with something such as a thought, having a conversation, or texting you are apt to lose focus on your surroundings. When you are observing, remember also not to use single-point focus. Rather, make maximum use of your peripheral vision, combining it with a slight head swivel to see your 270- to 360-degree blind spots. Do not stare at people who may concern you; be subtle with your observations.

Human eyes tend to focus on the obvious for good reason, but a seasoned observer will begin to look in, around, and between obvious concerns to survey an entire scene. Once you develop an awareness of your environment—any environment—you'll notice at all times who and what surrounds you. Fortunately, with minimal focused threat-recognition training, there is a good chance you'll spot trouble/danger and steer clear of it.

There are six different levels of awareness we refer to in Israeli krav maga:

-5	-4	-3	-2	-1	0
Unaware	Semi-aware	Aware	Cautious	Alert	Prepared

A large part of "awareness" is to understand your capacity and limits. What verbal or physical abuse you might accept or collectively what actions will cross your proverbial "redline" is obviously your decision. You must have a cache of predetermined decisions leading to decisive action based on the collective indicators and environment you observe. Note: An untrained fighter will size you up to decide if he can prevail. A seasoned fighter will decide how he intends to physicaly dominate you.

A surprise attack will force you to react from an unprepared state. You need to recognize a trap or an inchoate ambush. If a stranger springs out of nowhere, the attacker may have an accomplice flanking or lurking behind you. Train yourself with the mind-set of an attacker. Think how you would "get" or ambush yourself at any given moment and use that training to recognize potential dangers as you go about your daily life. When on the move and accosted by someone who arouses your suspicion, once again discard politeness and keep moving.

Be aware that there are threats who may mask their intent with charm. An attacker may feign social acquiescence and warmth with his palms open, friendly gestures, and a smile simply to psychologically disarm you and close the distance to better ambush you. A hand extended for a handshake can also draw you closer to control you. An attacker may also engage you in discussion to get you to look away or distract you and then pounce. So, for example, if you do stop to answer any questions, you should still remain vigilant watching the threat's entire body and keeping your distance. If you are blocked, spear your way through the person or people and hustle to safety.

As noted earlier in this chapter, author Rory Miller covers the predatory mind-set exceptionally well in his books. A predatory interview will begin by the aggressor closing in on you either to gauge how you will defend your personal space or to attack. Do not be polite. Your face should be resolute, but not scowling or sneering. Be prepared to act by positioning yourself and readying your "go" button. Scan the attacker's hands immediately and take a proper stance, noting quickly the environment around you. If you face down the threat and are prepared to act: (a) the attacker may be deterred and/or (b) you are prepared to now defend.

RECOGNIZING HOSTILE BODY LANGUAGE AND PRECONFLICT INDICATORS

When facing street violence, you can usually recognize verbal, behavioral, and physical manifestations indicating that violence is imminent. Recognize it or not—and it is decidedly advantageous that you do—it is highly likely there will be some indicator prior to an attack. When assessing body language, evaluating a potentially hostile person is best done in combination with his physical manifestations and words. Keep in mind though, that nonverbal gestures should be prioritized; these are strong indicators of someone's intentions and true feelings.

It is well understood that when verbal and nonverbal gestures do not align, nonverbal gestures usually take priority in predicting behavior. Nonverbal signaling often belies someone's true intent and is often manifested by "tells" or biological markers—body gestures, physical displays, and movements underpinning a person's mental state. Neural connections are most densely concentrated between the hands and the brain. Therefore, hand gestures may most directly indicate a person's emotional state, especially aggression. Thus, clenching one's fists is an obvious sign of aggression.

Successfully reading body language allows you to recognize a violent decision before the aggressor physically initiates it. For example, primates bare their teeth to attack or defend. Hence, sneering, which exposes one's teeth, is a hostile act by humans as well. Flaring one's nostrils provides more air intake to oxygenate the body for flight-or-fight. Lowering one's eyebrows also can signify forthcoming aggression (a primordial signal of dominance). Gross motor movements, including clenching one's hands and teeth, often signal hostile intention. A distinct flushing or pallor of the face, a forward lean, and other

KINESIC INDICATORS OF POSSIBLE VIOLENCE

Successfully reading hostile body language can allow you to recognize a violent decision before the aggressor physically initiates it. Gross motor movements often red flag someone who is adrenalized and about to explode. These movements may include a combination of the following nonexclusive twelve common tells or collective kinesic markers for you to anticipate an attacker's first salvo:

1. Fidgeting, shaking of one's limbs, muscle tremors, or clenching one's hands and teeth

2. Sweating, increased respiration or blinking excessively

3. A forward lean

4. Moving onto the balls of the feet in preparation to attack

5. Coiling a shoulder or blading the body

6. Stiffening the neck

7. Puckering the lips or sneering

8. A change in breathing (fast-paced or measured)

9. Puffing up (as the chest expands to intake as much oxygen as possible), becoming loud to intimidate, and turning red in the face and neck (vasodilations as blood fills the capillaries)

10. Becoming pale (vasoconstriction occurs as blood rushes from the skin surface to the internal organs), to indicate an advanced stage of fear or girding oneself against an attack and is one of the surest indicators someone is preparing for violence

11. Pupillary constriction toward something considered a threat or challenge along with momentary pupillary dilation, to indicate the very moment a person is ready to act

12. Disrobing to free the arms (and legs)

indicators red flag someone adrenalized and about to explode (see above box).

Importantly, pupil activity functions independently of conscious control and is associated with mental activity. When someone sees something he dislikes, the person's pupils usually constrict. When someone reaches a conclusion or decides to act or is surprised, the pupils dilate significantly for a moment. If an event is quickly processed as

IMPENDING VIOLENCE USUALLY HAS
OVERT OR COVERT SIGNALS

Many people who suddenly become embroiled in a violent encounter have no idea why it happened. Often, there is a buildup they did not recognize or were party to without their knowledge. A few common-sense suggestions:

- Be careful of other people's personal space.

- Do not return challenging stares or comments.

- Be aware of kinesic indicators indicating an angry or hostile person. (See previous box)

- If in the wrong, apologize sincerely, but be subtly prepared for a potential attack.

- Leave any volatile or potentially hostile situation immediately.

- Social mores, for women especially, should readily be ignored (for example, leave an elevator if you feel threatened by someone; don't worry about the person's feelings).

negative or hostile, the pupils change from dilated to constricted in a fraction of a second to see clearly and accurately to escape or defend. Recognizing pupillary oscillation can be difficult, especially with dark eyes. But it is still a telling phenomenon of possible aggression. Violence indicators also include recognizing a "give away" in a potential adversary's subtle physical movements or intuiting an energy shift. Physical changes result from an adrenaline dump just prior to action.

CONFLICT AVOIDANCE

Common sense and a few street smarts are your optimum weapons for de-confliction and to avoid violence. Truly understanding the nature and consequences of injurious violence should eliminate it as a dispute resolution option. Mental conditioning and rehearsal allows you to de-escalate or walk away (always the best solution if possible) from a potentially violent situation. In short, avoidance is often about keeping your cool, but so is every other aspect of self-defense, including de-escalation, escape and evasion, and, lastly, fighting for your life.

CONFLICT DE-ESCALATION

The key to avoiding social violence is not to provide provocations. An example might be not returning challenging or antagonistic stares or comments. Conversely, though, you can present vulnerability when avoiding eye contact by looking down and away, as you may project possible submission. The solution when confronted with a hard stare may be to look to the side to signal a level of nonconfrontational equanimity. If you do not believe a problem can be resolved by diplomacy or conciliation, use common sense—remain silent and disengage. In short, avoid eye contact or conversation with a potential aggressor; nip the situation in the bud. Another tactic is to project confidence, but this can also escalate matters. So, you must, of course, be capable of physically backing it up. Confidence projection can reflect being disinterested or simply nonplussed by the situation. Contrariwise, projecting nervousness suggests you consider yourself to be subordinate, which may provide the would-be aggressor additional underlying confidence to escalate.

Humans have a keen sense of power and powerlessness. Maintain your calm and try to respond rationally. There is a crucial difference in trying to appease someone whom you have bumped into versus using social skills to dissuade someone intent on punching you in the face. Many people straddling the fence between simply posturing or committing a violent act generally need a rationalization to justify the violent act. Do your best to talk the aggressor out of it, at the very least, do not give the aggressor a provocative response. Someone who is clearly in the wrong, but who will not admit his error, is likely to perceive any nonacquiescence as a personal insult or attack.

Blunt honesty may be one of the surest ways to defuse or de-escalate a situation—provided your would-be attacker is rational. If you made a mistake or are in the wrong, provide a credible apology, and leave. Keep in mind that appeasement or flattery with a predator also may not work. Such a strategy may inflame the aggressor further raising the level of the aggressor's violent onslaught. Another proven tactic to de-escalate a situation may be changing the context by, perhaps, injecting a non sequitur to make the aggressor think in a different direction. Think of a change-the-subject strategy you may have used to calm a small child (provided the troubling subject you know to be inconsequential). This change-of-subject tactic does not suggest that you infantilize a verbal de-escalation attempt for obvious reasons. Be sure your tone is not condescending. You

Deflecting Staring Challenges

Generally, in a social setting, the accepted average gaze length is just a few seconds; any longer and emotional intent is implied. Usually, the "subordinate" person looks away first. Nevertheless, when surveying a scene, do not hold eye contact. Break eye contact by looking sideways and not down as looking down may depict you as underconfident.

Deflecting Verbal Challenges

If forced into a potentially adversarial conversation, one strategy is to respond with laconic politeness. Avoid showing any unease that might mark you as either a challenge or target. Be aware that saying something that you believe to be innocuous may, paradoxically, be considered highly inflammatory by someone else, putting you in the crosshairs of violence. If an apology is demanded, do it sincerely and then immediately leave to defuse the situation. Attacking one's masculinity or femininity is a time-proven provocation. So, think about how you would respond to such a situation ahead of time as part of your mental training. If someone is hell-bent on a fight and accuses or challenges you, there may be no way to defuse the situation. A last-ditch approach may be to engage the individual, acknowledging his concern by stating something like, "Sorry, I had a tough day and certainly did not mean any offense."

As a personal example, I successfully de-escalated a potentially volatile situation on a Newark, New Jersey, train platform by cooing over a baby in a stroller. For whatever reason, a hard-bitten–looking individual with several tears tattooed on his face took exception with me as we collectively waited for a train to arrive. The would-be tough guy used the classic bait of "What are you looking at?" followed immediately by "You got a problem with me?"

My response was, "Is that your beautiful little girl?" He defensively said, "Yes." I sincerely reinforced my complimentary observation, "She is absolutely beautiful. How old is she?" With my unexpected verbal tactic, the father's demeanor transformed immediately as he beamed and told me the little girl was thirteen months. The baby's mother also smiled and seemed to breathe a sigh of relief. I ended up holding the train doors open for the couple and helping them board with the stroller. So, rather than face an ugly situation, I made some cursory friends. Author Rory Miller covers this topic well in his books *Facing Violence, Meditations on Violence,* and *ConCom: Conflict Communications.*

Verbal Self-Defense (Resolute Warning)

Forced civility can be the greatest undermining factor when successfully facing down potential violence. A hostile action can be preempted by issuing a resolute warning that you will respond with overwhelming counterviolence. But this approach poses the obvious risk of provoking the other party and/or escalating the situation. Resolutely tell any threat to get back, while maintaining strong eye contact. A short declarative statement sends the message, while clueing in other witnesses/bystanders. There is no need to explain yourself further than repeating the message with increasing emphasis. Be quasi-polite, but determinedly firm. Blade your body with your hands at the ready position with your palms facing the threat (see page 47).

may be able to derail his verbal aggression by deflecting an insult or challenge by an innocuous or conciliatory change-of-subject response. Remember, your attacker is experiencing an adrenaline dump and may not hear your attempts to defuse the situation. When an aggressor is adrenalizing, your ability to reason with the aggressor diminishes as the aggressor's nervous system goes into internal overload. Accordingly, the aggressor does not process your words; if he partially processes your words, obviously, your attempt to reason with him may be heard selectively.

You may also wish to switch tactics and paraphrase your initial attempt to reason with the potential aggressor. Yet, do not think too much; you may have to react instantaneously to an attack. Another de-escalatory tactic might be to walk up to a would-be aggressor and amiably introduce yourself to change the dynamic (again, be prepared to defend yourself if necessary). Always bear in mind that in a truly unavoidable violent situation, your de-escalation skills and social values are useless. Worse, these social conventions and rational behavior may prevent you from defending yourself at the inception of an attack, providing an attacker with an all-important vulnerable opening to hurt, injure, or kill you.

Personal Space Violations

Dominant-minded people often use their bodies to take ownership of more physical space. Examples include someone spreading out across a subway bench, or an airline seat/row; taking up most of the sidewalk when walking; or purposefully taking up two parking spaces to separate his or her car. Naturally, most people expect others to maintain a proper or respectful distance. (Note: Different cultures have different expectations.) When someone invades your personal or intimate space, your limbic warning system is immediately triggered as it recognizes the interloper is now within attack range of you. (Note: A firearm or other type of projectile weapon poses a longer-range threat.) Once again, if your gut sends an alarm signal, eschew social politeness, retreat if necessary, and tell the would-be aggressor to move away, while blading yourself. Watch a potential adversary's hands as you issue a warning to him. If the potential adversary objects to your demand to "back off," beware that this might just be the excuse he wanted to escalate matters. Be sure, once again, to understand the difference between an assertive versus a belligerent response. The former will let someone know in a matter-of-fact way to give you space. The latter may be considered an overreaction on your part that might worsen matters.

ESCAPING VIOLENCE

Escape methods are a vital and significant part of the krav maga curriculum. Escape is your second choice when avoidance and de-escalation fail. Escape is different from avoidance as the aggressor has already begun his actions and you are actively fleeing. (To review, avoidance allows you to calmly remove yourself before a hostile situation begins.)

To escape, your goal is to evade physical contact and preserve your ability to successfully flee. Your ultimate goal is to find safety through breaking contact and losing any pursuers by quickly hiding or finding safety among other people. Physically escaping requires you to recognize egresses and to successfully negotiate terrain and obstacles. For example, in a potential road rage incident, consider your driving escape options. (You should always leave enough room in front of your vehicle to maneuver.)

Terrain can aid or hamper you. High ground such as a stairwell gives you the advantage of gravity and using your strongest personal weapons: kicks. Conversely, when fleeing up a stairway, ascending it will slow you down as you take the first steps and pursuers can close the distance. Your footing, and hence your traction and balance, can be affected by liquids (including blood), gravel, wet grass, mud, snow, and ice. Therefore, you must both consciously and instinctively pay attention to your movements shifting your balance onto the balls of your feet and altering your stance/paces. Even if you disable an attacker through counterassault, the attacker may have accomplices. The accomplices may be shocked by your counterviolent actions, providing you with a head start.

When running away, seek the safety of other people, using concealment as available. (Note that professional escape and evasion requires preplanned evacuation routes, safe houses, and dedicated support, along with a number of other facets.) When running, focus on the physical route ahead of you. If you are part of a group, you must all act in concert: flee or fight together, acting as a cohesive unit. If you decide to flee, when favorable, you can also turn around to ambush your pursuer(s). In a road rage scenario, if you find yourself outside of your own vehicle (a tactical choice), you could momentarily escape an aggressor by running around the perimeter your own car. In a run-around-a-stationary-car scenario, you can also use preemptive self-defense (a counterambush) against the aggressor by swiftly changing directions and catching the would be assailant by surprise. However, if there are multiple pursuers, fighting a group is obviously not the best option.

THE SUBCONSCIOUS MIND LARGELY GOVERNS YOUR REACTION TO A VIOLENT ASSAULT

If you are about to fight someone, you will likely feel uncomfortable and, perhaps, frightened. Violent conflict produces severe stress on the human mind, slowing down the cognitive process. For our purposes, the human brain can be divided into two sections: the subconscious mind (limbic system) and the conscious mind (cerebral cortex system).

The subconscious mind governs our primordial survival mechanisms by reacting rather than "thinking." The subconscious mind searches for past experience in a dangerous situation for a suitable response. While serving as the emotional center, the subconscious mind controls physical reactions (as opposed to actions). Subconscious reactions, "thinking without thinking," are decided within the first nanosecond of a threat. This is the premise behind krav maga's instinctive movements/tactics.

The conscious mind is our higher brain. It is chiefly responsible for higher cognition and analysis. The conscious mind engages when you have the time to assess a situation thoroughly and respond deliberately. When you are caught off guard and are overwhelmed with stress, your conscious mind shuts down. All decision-making processes transfer to your subconscious mind. As noted, your subconscious mind is basically an instinctive command response or a data bank of muscle memory.

Importantly, the conscious and subconscious minds can be in competition or at odds with one another regarding self-defense. Once again, the subconscious relies on the body's natural self-preservation actions. The conscious mind may try to make logical sense of an action or event, leading to freezing action. When emotionally aroused, a person may have difficulty thinking clearly, because his cognitive abilities are being suppressed by the subconscious brain, which has hijacked all cerebral functions. In other words, when overwhelming stress shuts down your cognitive or conscious mind, responsibility transfers to your subconscious mind. Instincts will always govern your cognitive response under stress.

If your subconscious mind has no concrete muscle memory stored to engage the immediate problem, it simply makes your body defend itself the best way it knows how. Often, this is a flinch reaction involving your throwing your arms up in front of your face and chest to protect the body's vital areas and crouching down to become a smaller target. If your subconscious muscle memory cannot summon an instinctive response, your conscious mind will still make your body respond with its own primitive defenses.

"I saw my life flash in front of my eyes." Many people experience this response when they are in a dangerous situation where they believe they are about to die. This response happens for a very specific reason that is geared to help us survive under stress. The reason you see your life flash in front of your eyes is simple. If your subconscious mind has no proper muscle memory stored, it is confounded with no solution. Your subconscious mind scans the entire data bank of your life; from the day you were born to the present second, to evaluate if you were ever in a similar situation and how you responded. If there was a similar or parallel situation, your subconscious mind will take that same survival mode response and implement it in the current situation to make you survive.

An assailant's action of initiating an attack generally precedes a defender's reaction. In other words, action usually beats reaction (unless preemptive self-defense is employed by recognizing the impending attack before the aggressor has time to effectively launch it). Therefore, reducing the time from recognition to reaction is paramount in a defensive violent encounter. It bears repeating: Instincts will always govern your cognitive response under stress. Krav maga hones these instincts in recognizing that action will usually beat reaction in the action/reaction power curve. In other words, if an assailant launches at you, he has the initiative. You need to catch up. But you can and usually must "cheat" by recognizing kinesic indicators. For example, as noted previously on pages 22–23 if you see or are confronted by someone who is clenching his hands and teeth, moving onto the balls of his feet with a forward lean, coiling a shoulder, blading the body, or stiffening the neck, these are individual or collective kinesic indicators that he may be primed to attack.

Cortisol is a stress hormone, which, when released in a significant dose, will impair memory and make it difficult to remember things that are not deeply ingrained. Importantly, the longer a victim remains ensconced in fear, the longer it will take for the victim to recover/react. Crucially, the subconscious mind narrows the gap between reaction and action on the action/reaction power curve. Stated alternatively, the subconscious mind cannot be cognitively controlled. Hence, the importance of an instinctive/conditioned response for self-defense.

Instinctive (re)action harnesses adrenaline. As a result, the subconscious mind reverts to three simple seriatim processes:

1. **Freeze**

2. **Flight**

3. **Fight**

Freezing is an evolutionary process humans (and animals) developed to avoid a predator noticing them. Freezing is also the higher brain's attempt to take control of the situation. This survival mechanism is well illustrated by survivors playing dead during the Mumbai, Virginia Tech, and Paris shooting massacres. If the freeze process is not the optimum response, the limbic brain orders flight or escape. If flight is impossible, the subconscious brain's final mandate is to fight by converting apprehension and fear into violent fury.

If the conscious mind overcomes instinct to dictate a thought-out response, two additional outcomes may occur:

1. **Posing**

2. **Surrender**

Posing or posturing that you present a hard target or credible counterthreat may convince an aggressor to back down. Alternatively, it might spiral matters into physical violence. Surrender places you at an aggressor's mercy. This is both a tactical and strategic decision fraught with peril. You are submitting to an aggressor's intent (unless you are feigning acquiescence to counterattack at an opportune or optimum time).

Therefore, the freeze/flight/fight self-defense process may be understood using the following four-step process:

1. **THREAT RECOGNITION. In analyzing a potentially violent situation, the mind must recognize the danger and then process it.**

2. **SITUATION ANALYSIS. Once the mind recognizes the danger, it contemplates the possible outcomes and takes in any additional clues that may be helpful in arriving at a choice of action.**

3. **CHOICE OF ACTION. After processing the danger's potential outcome or outcomes, the mind quickly contemplates available courses of action and chooses one. This leads to the final stage, action/inaction.**

4. **ACTION/INACTION. After the mind settles on a reaction, it propels the body into action or the paralysis of inaction.**

Training "hardwires" your brain to move your body instinctively to bypass conscious thought and streamline the self-defense process. The key is to expedite or even eliminate steps (1) and (2) above. Additionally, people often freeze during step (1) by denying they are about to be caught in a violent maelstrom. Training's goal is to streamline each of the four steps collectively, making the process first nature. Safety is a primordial concern. So, trust your enhanced training instincts to trigger your defensive actions.

HUMAN EMOTIONAL AND PHYSICAL RESPONSES IN A LIFE-THREATENING ENCOUNTER

Unfamiliarity with violence obviously makes facing aggression a frightening prospect. Yet, coming to grips with the animalistic concept of damaging another human's anatomy is the foundation of effective self-defense. Both anxiety and subsequent fear, when triggered in a potentially violent situation, protect the body. Adrenalized strength is summoned, along with a heightened internal first-aid capability.

When confronting a life-threatening situation, shock can be more of a problem than fear. If you go into shock while under attack, you will freeze and not do anything. The reason victims go into shock when attacked is a lack of response preparation. To avoid going into shock under stress, constantly visualize yourself in every possible attack situation you may find yourself in. Optimally, you will act without thinking, using a conditioned/reflexive response. Train yourself over and over in your mind until you have effective solutions for those situations.

Fear triggers certain automatic human responses, including physical, emotional, perceptual, and cognitive—triggering the freeze/flight/fight reaction. Fear creates time and distance distortions where actions may be perceived to speed up or slow down. Fear, when transformed to panic, can also paralyze. Paradoxically, the human mind may ignore danger, when the body is instinctively reacting otherwise. Cognition, or an attempt at reason, may override the instinctive recognition of danger. The key is to transition immediately from surprised/fearful to a krav maga counter-assault mind-set. The following are some well-documented human responses in a violent situation of which you must be aware:

- **TUNNEL VISION. Under extreme stress, to increase blood and oxygen delivery to your eyes your attention may be focused primarily on the greatest threat, resulting in a temporary lost of peripheral vision.**

- **AUDITORY EXCLUSION. As your vision takes over, your hearing will diminish.**

- **TIME AND SPACE COMPRESS (TACHYPSYCHIA). Time and space will become muddled, with added difficulty in judging the interrelationship of speed and distance. Movements may appear in slow-motion.**

- **RANDOM DISTRACTING THOUGHTS CAN OCCUR. Your brain struggles with itself to prevent conscious decision making from interfering with primordial flight-or-fight mechanism.**

- **BEHAVORIAL LOOPING. May occur whereby you repeat an action again and again, while denying that the attack is actually happening. You may delude yourself by not seeing something—however harmful—so you do not have to face it, which can get you immediately maimed or killed.**

KRAV MAGA'S APPROACH TO FACING DOWN UNAVOIDABLE VIOLENCE

Krav maga's goal is to embed your subconscious reaction with the proverbial "(I have) been there, done that (through a training scenario)." Often, regardless of how hard or "realistically" you train, your subconscious mind knows the difference between training and reality. Denial is the most common obstacle to taking appropriate action. Often, with an untrained mind and body, it's difficult to process or accept that someone else intends you serious bodily harm. An assailant may know this and achieve his purpose accordingly. Krav maga training will prepare you, most importantly, with the mind-set and accompanying physical skills you need to prevail against any onslaught. Speed, economy of motion, and the appropriate measure of counterviolence will be ingrained in you. Realistic training helps to alleviate fear, panic, and other sensations as you prepare your body and mind to take the proper course of action, but they must never be mistaken for a real attack.

Krav maga founder Imi Lichtenfeld designed krav maga for people of all shapes, sizes, ages, and physical abilities. Training must attempt to simulate a real attack for you to understand the speed, ferocity, and strength a determined attacker may direct at you. Imi understood that actual violence differs greatly from choreographed training. Martial artists who have devoted many years to training have catastrophically found their skills inapplicable when facing a violent "street smart" attacker in a volatile violent environment.

To avoid freezing under pressure, you must train under pressure. To begin, for example, practice with a training partner or trusted friend. Direct your partner to simulate attack situations using extreme control. Do the mock attacks and corresponding defenses at half-speed to stay safe and avoid injury. (I recommend learning these sparring techniques under a qualified Israeli krav maga instructor, if possible.) Only as you develop control and a working familiarity with both the tactics and your training partner can you begin to move at full speed. Remember, the moves are designed to neutralize an attack at its inception. If practiced without caution or incorrectly, you can easily injure your training partner. As your training quickly advances, your tactics must work against determined resistance. Therefore, realism must be injected into your krav maga training. For example, with proper safety training equipment and under a qualified krav maga instructor's supervision, punches and kicks must eventually be thrown at 100% speed and power in multiple salvos. The strikes must be retracted quickly and not held out, telegraphed, or overexaggerated. Similarly, chokes, grabs, and takedowns should be performed with full speed and power yet under controlled conditions.

Most important, krav maga develops a paramount fighting attitude. People will generally not escalate if they are not convinced that they can get away with it. Evident self-doubt may provide a potential aggressor the edge, especially if the aggressor was ambivalent about escalating matters. Note again that certain body language, such as hangdog neck, slouching shoulders, nervous fidgeting, biting your lips, cowering, etc., can paint you as an easy victim.

Looking your would-be aggressor in the eyes, along with your body language, conveying the message, "I am not a victim," can meet the potential threat head-on. Strategically, however, such posturing may inflame the situation. If krav maga is necessary, summon the courage and determination to fight for your life. As noted, when you find yourself within a crisis situation, you will automatically feel an explosive mixture of adrenaline, fear, panic, and, perhaps, fury.

Mental and physical conditioning allows you to stave off panic and channel your adrenaline into action. Simultaneous mental dominance over both your fear and/or misgivings and your attacker provides a decisive advantage in a violent encounter. Believe that your training will carry the day regardless of an attacker's physical size, or possession of a weapon or if the attacker has accomplices. Yet, confidence must not lead to overconfidence. Do not underestimate any attacker and always expect the unexpected. Perhaps, most important, mental conditioning will also allow you to de-escalate or walk away (always the best solution if possible) from a potentially violent situation.

PREDATORY AMBUSH METHODS

Similar to animal predators, human predators often wait in ambush. Like animals, humans can also sense danger and fear in their prey or victim. Attackers may close on the victim immediately, using a surprise violent ambush or pseudo-charm to put the intended victim at ease, and then strike. Criminals often work in groups to surround, herd, surprise, distract, or simply overwhelm the victim. A favored method is to corner the victim by trapping the victim in a confined space with no escape. In either case, the aggressor uses a victim's obliviousness or some form of concealment to launch a surprise attack. In pressing an ambush, the attacker avails himself of shock and temporary paralysis to gain the advantage. The attacker chooses the time and place or the conditions most opportune for the attacker to put you in the "-5." Keep in mind that the average person can unleash four or more blows per second. Also, be keenly aware that more than 85 percent of the world's population is right-side dominant. Therefore, there is more than an 85 percent chance that an attack will be initiated from an aggressor's right side.

FIVE ELEMENTS OF AN AMBUSH

1. When an ambush is executed, the victim is usually distracted, complacent, outnumbered, or caught in a state of maximum unpreparedness ("-5").
2. The chances of escape for the victim are minimized or nonexistent, as the attacker has chosen the site and circumstances.
3. The attacker often acts from concealment or closes on the unwitting victim.
4. The attacker affords himself the chance and avenue for escape.
5. The attacker possesses the intent—and usually the capability—to physically dominate the victim.

REACTING TO AN ATTACK

An attack launched by surprise will force you to react from an unprepared state. Therefore, your self-defense reaction must be instinctive and reflexive. Krav maga training prepares you for just that. Your subconscious mind will turn your instinctive-trained responses into immediate action. Instinct assumes control. One time-tested solution to prepare the body and mind for conflict is to breathe in slowly and deeply through your nose and exhale through your mouth. One suggested method is to inhale counting "one-one thousand, two-one thousand, three one-thousand" and exhale using the same "one-one thousand, two-one thousand, three one-thousand" count.

If an aggressor has violent intent, you must have superior counterviolent intent. The four pillars of krav maga self-defense are: (1) awareness, (2) avoidance, (3) de-escalation, escape, and (4) last-resort decisive, simultaneous defense and attack. Notably, adrenaline dumps may benefit untrained students more than the body's coping mechanism of trained students. For the trained student, when ambushed, there is a choice of tactics rather than simply relying on defensive instincts. And a choice may impede a defender's reaction time (Hick's law).

SELF-DEFENSE TACTICS: AN OVERVIEW

The sooner you spot a potential aggressor, the more time you will have to act. A few instinctive tactics will enable you to survive the most common onslaughts. As the next chapters will show, the krav maga fighting system is designed to work against any type of aggressor. It cannot be overemphasized that the essential element is your mind frame: intention governs action. True self-defense focuses not simply on survival, but also on how to optimally hurt, injure, cripple, maim, and, if necessary, kill. Make the decision now to use counterviolence as a necessary last-resort tool. Reconcile any ethical limitations ahead of time. Understand your own triggers; what abuse/wrongs you will accept and what you won't accept. Until you are physically assaulted, you still have the aforementioned options of avoidance, de-escalation, and escape.

In krav maga, you will learn a few core techniques that you can perform instinctively and apply to myriad situations. You will learn how to protect your vital points and organs while simultaneously targeting the aggressor's vulnerable anatomy. If the situation requires, krav maga will teach you how to maximize the damage you can inflict by striking, kneeing, kicking, chopping, gouging, choking, dislocating joints, breaking bones, and taking your attacker down to the ground.

Crucially, self-defense is defending your body—not your ego or pride. The goal of krav maga training may be analogous to learning how to ride a bike: once you learn, you don't forget. Once again, only use counterviolence when you have no choice. If there be no nonviolent solution, proceed with extreme prejudice until you end the violent confrontation on your terms. While you cannot underestimate the attacker's ability, the paradox is that the attacker's skills, in the end, are irrelevant, as overcoming the threat is solely dependent on your intent and determination combined with correct combative anatomical targeting. In a preemptive self-defense situation, the sooner you neutralize the threat, the less chance the aggressor will have to dominate you.

Fight positioning determines your tactical advantage. Optimally, a kravist, or skilled krav maga fighter, will move quickly to a superior and dominant position relative to his attacker, known in krav maga parlance as the dead side. Dead side often provides you with a decisive tactical advantage. This strategy should revolve around your capabilities and preferred tactics involving long, medium, and short combatives combined with evasive maneuvers. Positioning becomes even more important when facing multiple attackers. Once superior position is achieved, the attacker will have a minimal ability to defend or to counter your retzev attack. Remember that retzev, by its nature of using all parts of your body and incorporating facets of a fight, provides an overwhelming counterattack.

Fights involve different phases that are best categorized by the distance or proximity attackers maintain as the fight progresses. From a long or medium range, fighters have

When facing multiple attackers, you must only engage only one at a time, using optimum combatives/ movement, while putting that attacker between you and any others. Inexperienced attackers, will, fortunately, group together. If you use correct tactical positioning by lining the attackers up one behind the other (never putting yourself between two attackers), you limit the attackers' abilities to harm you. There is a limitation on how many attackers can occupy the same space to get at you. In select circumstances you may have to go through them.

unhindered movement to batter one another, usually involving long kicks, medium punches, and other hand strikes. From a short range, knees, elbows, headbutts, and biting become options. This includes a variety of standing entanglements involving medium and short strikes, trapping, clinching, throws, takedowns, and standing joint locks combined for "close retzev." The final ground phase occurs when both fighters lock up to unbalance one another to the ground, involving medium and short combatives combined with locks and chokes.

Movement on the ground is different from standing movement. The nature of ground fighting can allow one attacker superior control and positioning: the other attacker cannot run or evade as he might while standing. Krav maga ground survival is best defined as "what we do up, we do down" with additional specific ground-fighting capabilities. Krav maga employs many of its standing combatives on the ground including groin, eye, and throat strikes in combination with joint breaks and dislocations designed to maim your attacker.

Footwork and body positioning, whether standing or prone, allow you to simultaneously defend and attack, leading to seamless combative transitions essential to retzev. The key to evasion is moving out of the "line of fire" or the path of an attacker's offensive combatives. Clearly, positioning yourself where you can counterattack your attacker more easily than the attacker can attack you is most advantageous.

Human vision is limited by blind spots. You cannot see what is behind you (hence the effectiveness of rear ambushes). Even when looking straight ahead, you cannot see your feet. Therefore, a low-line kick may come in "under the radar." Tactically, straight-line attacks are more difficult to recognize and, therefore, to defend. Moreover, recall that

Essential to a successful defense is correct timing: using the appropriate tactic at the correct time. Fight timing is harnessing instinctive body movements while seizing or creating opportunities to defend both effectively and logically. Alternatively defined, fight timing is the defender's ability to either capitalize on a window of opportunity offered by the adversary or to create his own injurious opportunity, using whatever tactics come instinctively to end the confrontation. Preemption and fight timing are an instantaneous fusion of instinct and decision-making.

You have the choice to either preempt an opponent's attack by initiating your own attack or wait to be attacked to exploit and counterattack a physical vulnerability the opponent exposes. In other words, the opponent, even when skilled in delivering his attack, leaves himself briefly open for counterattack. For example, as the opponent delivers a straight punch, he shifts his weight forward offering you the opportunity to deliver a side kick to damage his front knee.

Timing must be developed and sharpened with realistic training—always krav maga's objective. While speed is not timing, speed can deliver a decisive advantage when the defender acts more quickly than the assailant. Krav maga relies on economy of motion to eliminate wasted movement, which, in turn, improves speed.

the fastest route between two points is a straight line, thus the effectiveness of linear combatives. Outside attacks such as hooks and roundhouse kicks are more recognizable, because these looping attacks break the attacker's silhouette and must travel approximately three times as far to reach a target.

Trained defenders look for the mental commitment and corresponding physical manifestations noted previously, such as blood draining from an attacker's face, increased breathing, and a subtle weight shift forward before the actual physical attack. One strong indicator is a head-to-toe slight shudder as adrenaline pours into the attacker's system. If the attacker contracts rather than expands, you may be dealing with a trained fighter coiling to spring into action. While pupil dilation and constriction can indicate an impending attack, an experienced fighter may initiate his attack without demonstrating these phenomena precisely because the attacker has done it before. The attacker's actions might be practiced; they might have become second nature. Watch for shoulder and hip movements, which also allow a defender to instantaneously recognize an incoming attack.

BREAKING YOUR ATTACKER'S BODY

Developed as a military fighting discipline, krav maga employs lethal force tactics. These tactics are responsibly taught only to the military and professional security organizations. Honing the use of your own personal weapons (hands, forearms, elbows, knees, shins, feet, head, and teeth), while focusing on an attacker's vulnerabilities, is essential to krav maga fight strategy and tactics. Anatomical damage occurs when trauma damages tissue and bones. In short, injury breaks down human anatomical structure and function—the aggressor's ability to harm you. Therefore, physical injury inflicted against an adversary compromises both his ability to attack and defend. This, in turn, affords you the chance to impose further strategic injury through retzev. Keep in mind that, if the adversary sees his body being dismantled, he will likely suffer emotional trauma as well as further sapping of his will to keep attacking.

To be sure, certain attacks can be lethal, but the body can perform miraculous feats even when severely injured. The body's resilience works for both victim and assailant. Adrenaline is a powerful energizer and allows the body to momentarily insulate itself against pain. Note: an assailant under the influence of drugs acquires yet another layer of pain insulation and artificially increased strength.

While pain may stop some attackers, other individuals have enormous pain thresholds. Therefore, resolve ahead of time to physically impair or maim any attacker. Your goal, depending on the severity of the aggression or attack, is to produce either superficial or longer-term physical trauma or both, using the shortest possible path and time to disable the attacker. A unilateral paroxysm of counterviolence must work decisively in your favor. Target vulnerable anatomy, damage that anatomy, continue to damage it, and move on to the next anatomical target as necessary, until the attacker no longer poses a threat to you or others.

To stop an assailant, krav maga primarily targets the body's vital soft tissue, chiefly the groin, neck, and eyes. Other secondary targets include organs and bones such as the kidneys, solar plexus, knees, liver, joints, fingers, nerve centers, and other smaller fragile bones. Krav maga differs from self-defense systems that may rely primarily on targeting difficult-to-locate nerve centers. In the heat of a struggle, this type of precise combative is extremely difficult. Conversely, a krav maga combative to the groin is precise enough to debilitate the attacker and is simple to deliver.

The human body is affected by anatomical injury in a foreseeable manner. With training and a basic understanding of how the human body responds to trauma, you can generally predict how your counterattacks will affect the attacker's subsequent movements or capacity to continue violence against you. For example, if you knee someone in the groin, you are likely to drop the attacker's height level, thus exposing the base of the skull or the back of the neck to a vertical combative strike. When justifiable, administering sequential injurious physical trauma epitomizes the effective krav maga counterviolence of retzev.

24 VULNERABLE TARGETS

In krav maga, you learn to avoid hard skeletal bones such as the back of the head to focus your efforts on easy-to-strike soft tissues. Vulnerable targets include:[2]

1. Hair
2. Eyes
3. Temples
4. Base of the skull
5. Nose
6. Ears
7. Mouth
8. Chin and jaw
0. Throat (specifically the windpipe)
10. Sides, back, and hollow of the neck
11. Base of the neck
12. Clavicles
13. Elbows
14. Ribs
15. Solar plexus
16. Back and kidneys
17. Stomach
18. Fingers
19. Testicles
20. Thighs
21. Knees
22. Shin
23. Ankles
24. Top of the feet

2. Col. David Ben-Asher, *Fighting Fit: The Israel Defense Forces Guide to Physical Fitness and Self-Defense* (New York: Perigee Books, 1983).

Many people think of hand-to-hand combat as exactly that: using your fists to strike at an attacker. Yet, krav maga teaches you to use every practical part of your body—from the head to the foot—as tools to deliver strikes. Regardless of your body size or muscular strength, you can deliver powerful strikes with your hands and elbows (along with your lower body—covered in the next chapter). The power behind a combative strike optimally comes from deliberate execution, especially when placing your center mass (found just below your navel) behind the strike. Of course, body size and muscular strength help your combatives. Your striking limb should remain loose until just before impact to take maximum advantage of your fast twitch (up until a fraction of a second before contact) and slow twitch (at the moment of contact) muscle fibers respectively.

Precise execution of an upper-body or lower-body strike will generate greater impact than simply muscling your way through one. Physics dictates that acceleration times mass equals force. In other words, your strike will generate more force if you accelerate your speed as you extend your limb and put all of your body weight (center mass) behind the combative to deliver the maximum energy.

TWO

PUSH DEFENSES

AGGRESSION OFTEN BEGINS WITH A ONE- OR TWO-HANDED PUSH. THIS PROVOCA-

TION TYPICALLY MARKS AN AGGRESSOR'S ATTEMPT TO ASSERT SOCIAL DOMI-

NANCE OR TO GOAD YOU INTO A FIGHT. SOMEONE PUSHING YOU AWAY MAY ALSO BE

PRECIPITATED BY YOUR INVADING THAT PERSON'S SOCIAL SPACE. PUSH DEFENSES,

as with all krav maga defenses, involve the all-important krav maga concept of simultaneous defense and attack. As the defender, your preference is to move off the line of attack, in this case, the line of the attacker's push. One option is to simply sidestep and parry the push to let the aggressor move past you. Another option is to escalate matters using a decisive counterattack. The following are a few possible physical responses.

LEG-RANGE DEFENSES

Krav maga separates its defenses into two basic ranges: "legs" and "hands." Leg-range defenses are used when the attacker is farther away and the defender recognizes the assault early enough and with enough distance to use a straight kick (or side kick.) The key with leg-range defenses is using proper timing, target selection, and base-leg (nonkicking leg) movement to extend the hip and drive your body mass through the aggressor's targeted anatomy.

FRONT STRAIGHT KICK INTERCEPTION AGAINST A PUSH

The front straight kick option is a quick, highly effective option to intercept or preempt the attacker's ability to push you.

From a de-escalation stance, as you recognize the attacker begin to extend his arms, begin to pivot on the ball of the foot of your rear (right) leg. This pivot transfers your weight forward as you extend your forward (left) leg through the attacker's groin or midsection. As you deliver the straight kick, launch your left leg forward naturally as you would kick a bouncing ball. Do not pull your knee up abnormally and then thrust your leg out. Curl you toes and kick with the ball of your foot. Be sure to raise your arms up, as this helps pull your body weight forward while also placing you in a proper fighting stance to continue your counterattack as needed.

REAR STRAIGHT KICK INTERCEPTION
AGAINST A PUSH

Similar to the front kick option, you may use a rear kick to intercept or preempt the attacker's ability to push you. The rear kick generally provides more power, as you can generate more torque. Importantly, the rear kick requires the defender to have enough distance coupled with correct timing and attack recognition to fully extend the hip before the attacker can close or deliver the attack.

From your de-escalation stance, as you recognize the attacker begin to extend his arms, begin to pivot on the ball of the foot of your front (left) leg. This pivot begins to transfer your weight forward, as you extend your rear (right) leg through the attacker's groin or midsection.

As you deliver the straight kick, launch your right leg forward naturally as you would kick a bouncing ball. Once again, do not pull your knee up abnormally and then thrust your leg out. Curl you toes and kick with the ball of your foot. Be sure to raise your arms up, as this helps pull your body weight forward, while also placing you in a proper fighting stance to continue your counterattack as needed.

This drill requires two partners, P1 (the "Defender" [you]) and P2 ("Attacker" [your partner]). P1 faces P2 about three to six feet apart, simulating a confrontation where P2 initiates as the aggressor. Practitioners should repeat this drill a minimum of 15 repetitions per kicking leg (30 repetitions total).

1. Against P2's push attempt, P1 delivers straight front timing kicks at 25% power—not full force—to the midsection (not the groin for safety purposes) of P2 to simulate stopping an advancing attacker (P2). These are light kicks. P2 uses body absorption by tensing the midsection and abdominal muscles, while exhaling out strongly to create a vacuum, when the ball of P1's foot makes contact.

2. Against P2's push attempt, P1 delivers straight rear timing kicks at 25% power—not full force—to the midsection (not the groin for safety purposes) of P2 to simulate stopping an advancing attacker (P2). These are light kicks. P2 uses body absorption by tensing the midsection and abdominal muscles, while exhaling out strongly to create a vacuum when the ball of P1's foot makes contact.

3. This variation requires a suitable kicking pad or shield. Against P2's simulated push attempt (signaled by P2's physical movement toward P1) P1 delivers a straight front or rear timing kick, using 50% power against a walk at P1 by P2, 75% power against a light jog at P1 by P2, and 100% power against a run at P1 by P2. The pad holder (P2), should exhale on contact similar to step #1.

4. A variation of this drill could involve utilizing a hanging heavy bag. P2 stands behind the bag and pushes the bag forward to simulate an attacker's advance. P1 delivers various levels of power.

5. As you improve your skill set and capabilities, you may then bolster your defense by adding two kicks or a kick and then knee combination.

   a. A straight kick and same-side straight punch or palm heel combination. In other words, if you kick with your right leg as soon as your foot makes contact with the target, initiate a straight punch or palm heel strike followed by additional punches, elbow strikes, knees, kicks, etc.

   b. Rear kick and turn into straight kick variation to finish with retzev continuous combat motion counterattacks.

Note: A variation of this drill can be used to defend against your partner attacking with straight punches, hook/haymaker punches, grabs, and chokes.

HAND-RANGE DEFENSES

Hand-range defenses are used when the attacker is closer and the defender recognizes the assault with enough time to intercept or deflect the attack. Similar to leg-range defenses, the key is using proper timing, target selection, and moving on both balls of your feet to drive your body mass through the aggressor's targeted anatomy.

DEFLECTION WHEN YOUR HANDS ARE DOWN USING A GROIN STRIKE

This first hand-range defense may be used if you have your hands down in a passive stance. In other words, you are caught in the "-5" and did not recognize the aggressor's action until the last possible reaction moment before the aggressor attempts to push you.

From a passive stance, as you recognize the attacker begin to extend his arms, make a short pivot or quarter tai sabaki step with your rear leg as you blade your body to deflect the attacker's arms. In other words, you are making a quarter of a circle step with your rear right leg to take your body off the straight line of the push.

As you deflect the attacker's incoming arms with your upper triceps and shoulder, the attacker will continue to surge forward. Smash the attacker in the groin with a right underhand palm heel strike. Pivot on the ball of your rear foot for maximum power. If necessary, continue with additional retzev combatives to stop the attacker's aggression.

PUSH DEFENSE DRILLS USING ARM DEFLECTIONS AND BODY DEFENSES

This drill requires two partners, P1 (the "Defender" [you]) and P2 ("Attacker" [your partner]). P1 faces P2 about one to two feet apart, simulating a confrontation where P2 initiates as the aggressor. Practitioners should repeat this drill a minimum of 15 repetitions for each tactical variation (30 repetitions total).

1. Against P2's push attempt when P1's hands are down, P1 uses a body defense performed using the tai sabaki footwork. P1 avoids the push by deflecting with P1's arm/shoulder and delivers and counterattacks using a hand strike to P2's thigh (not the groin for safety purposes).

DEFLECTION WHEN YOUR HANDS ARE DOWN USING A KNEE STRIKE

This defense is identical to the first defense, Deflection When Your Hands Are Down Using a Groin Strike, you learned, but rather than counterstriking with your hand to the attacker's groin, use a modified roundhouse knee strike instead with your rear leg. From a passive stance, as you recognize the attacker begin to extend his arms, make a short pivot with your rear leg as you blade your body to deflect the attacker's arms (see page 51). As you deflect the attacker's incoming arms with your upper triceps and shoulder, the attacker will continue to surge forward. As you deflect the attacker's arms, knee the attacker in the groin with your rear leg. As you propel your knee through the attacker's groin or midsection, be sure to raise your arms up into a proper fighting position. This helps accelerate your mass through the lower-body strike and prepares you, if necessary, to continue with additional combatives to stop any further aggression.

L PARRY/BLOCK AGAINST A PUSH USING A COUNTERPUNCH

This defense may be used if you have your hands in a low ready position with your body bladed. This low ready position serves as both a de-escalation and prepared defensive position. By not raising your arms fully to your eyebrows in a defensive posture (thereby possibly demonstrating aggression to the aggressor [and witnesses]) with your palms up facing the aggressor, you appear to be in a "reasoning" position facing toward the aggressor. If the attacker uses one arm or two arms to push you, this position readily allows you to deflect the attacker's incoming arm(s), while also facilitating a body defense.

Rotate your front arm using a modified chop to deflect the attacker's incoming arms combined with a sidestep body defense. Importantly in krav maga, the hand always leads the body by intercepting or deflecting the incoming strike a fraction of a second before the combined body defense follows.

As the attacker extends his arms, maintain contact with the attacker's near-side arm enabling you to clamp down and control the arm. As you simultaneously begin to clamp down on the arm, strike the attacker with either a straight punch or palm heel to the attacker's jaw, ear, or temple.

Opposite view of punch counterattack to the head. Continue with additional retzev combatives as necessary.

L PARRY/BLOCK AGAINST A PUSH USING A KNEE STRIKE

This defense (not depicted in the photos) is identical to the previous initial defensive movements of using your forward arm rotation to deflect/attack the incoming push (see page 53), while stepping off the line of attack to immediately deliver a knee strike to the attacker's groin. This defense uses a strong knee strike to the attacker's groin or midsection. Once again, this defense may be used if you have your hands in a low ready position with your body bladed. If the attacker uses one arm or two arms to push you, this position readily allows you to deflect the attacker's incoming arm(s) while also facilitating a body defense. Rotate your front arm using a modified chop to deflect the attacker's incoming arms combined with a sidestep body defense. As the attacker extends his arms past you, transition your weight onto your front leg, preparing to deliver your modified roundhouse knee counterattack. Drive your kneecap (patella) through the attacker's groin or midsection. Continue with additional retzev counterattacks as necessary.

PUSH DEFENSE DRILLS USING ARM DEFLECTIONS AND BODY DEFENSES

This drill requires two partners, P1 (the "Defender" [you]) and P2 ("Attacker" [your partner]). P1 faces P2 about one to two feet apart simulating a confrontation where P2 initiates as the aggressor. Practitioners should repeat this drill a minimum of 15 repetitions for each tactical variation (30 repetitions total).

1. Against P2's push attempt, P1, from a low ready bladed stance, uses an L block/parry deflection combined with a body defense performed using tai sabaki footwork. P1 deflects the push with a correct arm rotation (mini inside chop) to deliver light counterattacks using an open hand to P2's head (remember anatomical combative targeting in a real situation).

2. Against P2's push attempt, P1 uses an L block/parry deflection combined with a body defense performed using the tai sabaki footwork. P1 deflects the push with a correct arm rotation (mini inside chop) to deliver a light modified straight knee to P2's thigh (not the groin for safety purposes).

SIDESTEP INTO AN ARM LOCK

This defense may be orchestrated from your low ready position and relies on correct timing to side-step the attacker's push and lock the attacker's extended arm out. The underlying principle of a joint lock is to force or hyperextend the joint, the elbow joint in this case, beyond its natural range and articulation. Importantly, think about what you will do with someone once you have him "locked" down or up as the case may be. Decide how you will de-escalate the situation. Will you yell for someone to call the police? Will you try to calmly tell the aggressor to calm down and, if so, will you let the aggressor go? Keep in mind you can be charged with "false imprisonment," if you detain someone against his will. Of course, in this case, the aggressor pushed you, but you must always beware of liability in the use of self-defense.

As the attacker begins to extend his arm(s) to push you, raise your arms above the attacker's. Using a correct tai sabaki sidestep and body defense, allow the attacker's arm to graze your torso.

As the attacker fully extends his near-side "push" arm, snatch the attacker's arm with your rear arm, securing the attacker by the attacker's wrist as your rotate your front arm over the top of the attacker's triceps. As you secure the attacker's arm, lean forward to begin exerting pressure on the back of the attacker's elbow. To complete the lock, step forward with your front leg while wrapping your near-side arm over the top of the attacker's arm and snaking it underneath it. Be sure to keep your torso glued to the attacker and not allow any bodily separation to optimize the lock. Finalize the lock by creating a figure-four hold with your near-side arm clamping down while grabbing the biceps of your other arm. Lean forward to apply severe pressure to the attacker's elbow fulcrum.

PUSH DEFENSE DRILLS USING ARM DEFLECTIONS AND BODY DEFENSES

This drill requires two partners, P1 (the "Defender" [you]) and P2 ("Attacker" [your partner]). P1 faces P2 about one to two feet apart, simulating a confrontation where P2 initiates as the aggressor. Practitioners should repeat this drill a minimum of 15 repetitions for each tactical variation (30 repetitions total).

- Against P2's push attempt, P1 uses a body defense performed using the tai sabaki footwork. Reacting from a low ready stance, P1 avoids the push while looping the near-side arm up and away. As P2 moves forward with the push attempt, P1 executes the arm bar. For safety purposes perform this drill at 25% speed, 50% speed, and 100% speed (being careful not to hyperextend your partner's elbow).

THREE

DEFENDING GRABS AND CHOKES

IF AN AGGRESSOR IS ABLE TO CLOSE THE DISTANCE ON YOU AND VIOLATE YOUR

PERSONAL SPACE, THE AGGRESSOR CAN GRAB OR CHOKE YOU. ONCE YOUR

ATTACKER GRABS YOU, THE ATTACKER CAN INFLICT A LIFE-THREATENING CHOKE

HOLD. OTHER TYPES OF CLOSE-CONTACT GRAPPLING INCLUDE HEADLOCKS AND bear hugs—each of which can put you in an extremely vulnerable position. Grabs and chokes are optimally defended using long-range preemptive linear kicks or upper-body strikes to prevent the attacker from seizing you. Against an arm or throat grab, you may also use the L Parry/Block Against a Push Using a Counterpunch (pages 54–55) depicted against a push to thwart someone's attempt to grab you by the arm or by the throat. If you do deflect his or her hands away, be prepared to counter-attack or to issue an unequivocal warning not to touch you.

If your preemptive strike defenses do not work and/or you were caught in the "-5" (you did not react in time), when secured by an aggressor who then pulls or pushes you, you must move with the push or pull. Initially, you may find that instinctively you wish to pull back or resist the momentum of the pull or push. Moving with the momentum, rather than resisting it, however, helps you to fight back to use your attacker's momentum against the attacker. In other words, by moving in the direction of the pull or push, you use the attacker's momentum against him, allowing your punches, elbows, kicks, knees, and headbutts to connect with greater force. This is just one of a handful of tactics that krav maga employs that may seem counter-instinctual, but, in reality makes great sense because it harnesses the attacker's momentum against him. For example, if an attacker grabs one of your arms, strike back with your free arm or one of your legs, targeting the attacker's vulnerable anatomy. As the attacker pulls you in one direction, move in the same direction to enhance these counterattacks. If your attacker still does not let go despite your barrage of strikes, you can employ an arm grab release to disengage yourself.

In a less aggressive and more de-escalation mode, krav maga employs direct releases to force your attacker to let go without injuring the attacker. The key is to find your attacker's grip's weakest angle and work against the thumb, the weakest digit. Do not work against the combined strength of your attacker's remaining four clutched fingers. Arm grab releases build the foundation for releases from a choke, one of the most life threatening methods of attack.

With practice, you will begin to recognize where the opening in an aggressor's grip is. You can then work against this with the help of your opposite arm to break a hold. To show this simple principle, bring your right thumb to your right index finger, creating a circle or an "okay" gesture. Insert your left thumb underneath and through the circle. If you had to create an opening in the circle with your left hand, you would not be able to do it by pushing against the web of your hand. Rather, you would have to pull it against the tips of your thumb and forefinger, the weak link in the circle. The same principle works to release arm grabs and choke holds. You will work against the attacker's thumb placement to break your attacker's grip.

Note: For all of the techniques presented in this chapter, were the attacker to grab your opposite arm with his opposite arm, you would simply mirror the technique and counterattack using the opposite side of your body (see *Krav Maga*, pages 115–17).

COMBATIVE STRIKES TO RELEASE FROM AN ARM GRAB

Combative releases from arm grabs are just that: use your strike arsenal to target the attacker's vulnerable areas. If the attacker pulls you, move in the direction of the pull and employ retzev combatives. If you do not feel your life is in danger, use gentler joint manipulation and pain compliance techniques that are not designed to produce damage to your attacker (see *Advanced Krav Maga*, pages 77–78).

ATTACKER GRABS YOUR LEFT ARM WITH HIS RIGHT— IMMEDIATE COMBATIVES OPTION #1

The attacker was somehow able to close the distance and secure your left arm with the attacker's right arm.

As the attacker pulls you, move with the attacker to harness both the attacker's momentum and your momentum to administer a combative of your choice. Eye gouges work well by bending your fingers and targeting your three middle fingertips into the attacker's eyes. (Do not keep the fingers straight, as you can jam or break them on impact.) Follow up with a strong knee to the attacker's groin. For the knee strike, be sure to fully extend your right hip by pivoting on the ball of the foot of your left "base" leg. Drive your weight through the target.

The attacker was somehow able to close the distance and secure your left arm with the attacker's left arm. Once again, as the attacker pulls you, move with the attacker to harness both the attacker's momentum and your momentum to administer a crippling side kick to the attacker's near-side knee. A side kick to the knee is one of krav maga's most effective counterattacks. As the attacker pulls you, raise your near-side left leg up by drawing your knee up to your waist.

As you deliver the left side kick, pivot on the ball of the foot of your right leg. Drive your heel through the attacker's knee, while leaning your upper body defensively away from the attacker. Continue your counterattacks as necessary and disengage, moving to safety.

This drill requires two partners, P1 (the "Defender" [you]) and P2 ("Attacker" [your partner]). P1 faces P2 about one to three feet apart simulating a confrontation where P2 initiates as the aggressor. Practitioners should repeat this drill a minimum of 15 repetitions for each tactical variation (30 repetitions total).

1. Against P2's arm grab, P1 (caught in the "-5") moves with the pull using P1's free arm to administer upper-body combatives to defeat the assault. Simulate various upper-body strikes such as straight punches and palm heels or other combatives against anatomical vulnerabilities, along with eye strikes. Use care and caution not to injure your partner.

2. Against P2's arm grab, P1 (caught in the "-5") moves with the pull using lower-body combatives such as straight kicks and knees along with side kicks to defeat the assault.

3. Against P2's arm grab, P1 (caught in the "-5") moves with the pull using P1's free arm to administer upper-body combatives combined with lower-body retzev combatives to defeat the assault.

4. This drill can also be performed with a hanging heavy bag, where P2 stands behind the bag and grabs P1. P1 reacts to the grab by attacking the bag, using retzev continuous combat motion counterattacks.

COMBATIVE STRIKES TO RELEASE FROM A SHIRT HOLD

Combative releases from shirt holds are just that: use your strike arsenal to target the attacker's vulnerable areas.

The attacker was able to somehow close the distance and grab your shirt. If the attacker pulls you, move in the direction of the pull while preparing to employ retzev combatives. If you do not feel your life is in danger, use gentler joint manipulation and pain-compliance techniques (not depicted) that are not designed to produce damage to your attacker (see *Advanced Krav Maga*, pages 77–78).

Harnessing the attacker's pull and your forward momentum, strike the attacker in the jaw, nose, throat, groin, or any other opportune anatomical target. Continue with your combatives. Note: Your step forward places your weight on your front left leg facilitating a rear right knee strike to the attacker's groin. Importantly, secure the attacker by the attacker's left shoulder to create a brace against the attacker's throat that protects you from receiving an inadvertent headbutt as you drive your knee through the attacker.

For maximum combative effect, be sure to pivot on the ball of your left base-leg foot (your nonkicking leg). Continue with additional combatives as necessary.

COMBATIVE STRIKES TO RELEASE FROM A SHIRT GRAB

This drill requires two partners, P1 (the "Defender" [you]) and P2 ("Attacker" [your partner]). P1 faces P2 about one to three feet apart, simulating a confrontation where P2 initiates as the aggressor. Practitioners should repeat this drill a minimum of 15 repetitions for each tactical variation (30 repetitions total).

1. Against P2's shirt grab, P1 (caught in the "-5") moves with the pull using P1's free arm to administer upper-body combatives to defeat the assault. Simulate various upper-body strikes such as straight punches and palm heels or other combatives against anatomical vulnerabilities, along with eye strikes. Use care and caution not to injure your partner.

2. Against P2's shirt grab, P1 (caught in the "-5") moves with the pull, using lower-body combatives such as straight kicks and knees along with side kicks to defeat the assault.

3. Against P2's shirt grab, P1 (caught in the "-5") moves with the pull, using upper-body combatives combined with lower-body retzev combatives to defeat the assault.

4. This drill can also be performed with a hanging heavy bag where P2 stands behind the bag and grabs P1. P1 reacts to the grab by attacking the bag, using retzev continuous combat motion counterattacks

FOUR

DEFENDING HOOK/ HAYMAKER PUNCHES

PASSIVE OUTLET STANCE

At times you may be caught by surprise while you are standing in a passive outlet stance. Most people do not stand in a regular outlet stance but rather in a passive outlet stance, when not expecting confrontation. In other words, you are standing with your feet parallel and your hands down. Of course, when possible, stand in your regular outlet stance at all times during a confrontation.

In the passive outlet stance, your feet are under your hips and your arms are at your sides. Although this stance is not a strong fighting stance, you should practice defenses and delivering strikes from this stance and moving from your passive outlet into a regular outlet in the event you are caught by surprise.

Place your feet close together with your toes facing forward. Rotate your toes counterclockwise as you turn your body 30 degrees to your right, coming into a left regular outlet stance with your left arm and left leg forward. (You can also turn 30 degrees to your left to come into a right regular outlet stance, so that your right leg and arm are forward.) Take a step back with the right foot until you feel comfortable and balanced. While keeping your right foot firmly planted, raise your back heel slightly and drop your body weight into the ball of your foot. Allow just enough separation between your rear heel and the ground to slide a piece of paper under your foot with your weight on both balls of the feet. Your feet should be parallel with about 55% of your weight distributed over your front leg. Raise your arms so that your hands are at your chest level, with your elbows kept close to your torso.

REGULAR OUTLET STANCE

Position your arms in front of your face and slightly forward. Extend your arms so your upper arms are parallel to the ground. Bend your elbows to form a 60-degree angle between your forearms and your upper arms. Hold your hands at eyebrow level, about six inches apart, but do not block your line of sight. For some trainees, especially those with large shoulders, this hand positioning can be uncomfortable. In this case, position the width of your hands as you feel comfortable but try to keep them within the width of your shoulders. Cup your hands with the fingers held together. Tuck your chin and look up toward your imaginary attacker. In a real fighting situation you will focus on the attacker's face as you retain an overall picture of the attacker's movements, especially the attacker's hands.

From this stance, you can move forward, laterally, and backward. Always stay and move on the balls of your feet, not on your heels. Practice your footwork and move in all directions. Your feet should always move in concert. Do not overextend yourself. Practice switching from a left regular outlet stance (with your left leg forward) to a right regular outlet stance (with your right leg forward). For example, from the left outlet stance a rear kick with the right foot will bring you forward into a right outlet stance. As you switch from one stance to another, keep your arms raised in your protective position. As your training progresses, you will be able to seamlessly move from one stance into another.

You may wish to stand in a de-escalation stance or low ready position, if you are concerned that someone near you may pose a threat. To help you not signal a provocative movement or fighting stance, keep your hands in front of you at sternum level, held in front of you with your palms facing the potential adversary.

RANGE AND DISTANCE REVIEWED

Range and distance are integral to your self-defense strategy. When defending against upper-body attacks, depending on the attacker's distance, a kravist may choose to employ "leg defenses" or close the distance immediately by using "hand defenses." You can kick an attacker if the attacker is in leg range or several feet away from you. Optimally, you can debilitate your attacker before the attacker can touch you, but such precision and timing is difficult. If the attacker has already closed the distance and is in physical contact with you, the attacker has entered your medium- and close-distance fighting ranges, in which case you must use upper-body defenses and combatives.

Regardless of the type of strike you deliver, remember to shift your body weight forward to deliver your combative strike. That allows you to place all of your body weight behind the combative strike, connecting with greater force. Here are some review pointers for striking effectively: In short, for, optimum striking capability, drive your combined body mass and collective force through an adversary's vulnerable anatomy, using correct pivoting and weight displacement.

BODY DEFENSES, MOVEMENT, AND ABSORPTION AGAINST PUNCHES

No matter how much you train and become proficient with defenses, there is a good chance you could still get hit. This is especially true if an attacker were to catch you unaware or in the "-5" with your hands down. Therefore, you must train your body to move with and absorb strikes. When receiving a blow to the head, move your head with the direction of the strike to the best of your ability. Do not tense and strengthen your neck to meet or resist the strike. This will only increase the strike's impact.

With body shots to your torso, you must create a vacuum by exhaling and strengthening your abdominal muscles. By exhaling on impact, you will avoid having the wind knocked out of you. In addition, tensing your midsection allows you to better withstand the strike. Try moving and absorbing your partner's light controlled strikes with your eyes closed to make these drills more instinctive. Ask your partner to strike lightly at you as you practice moving with the strike, tightening your abdomen and exhaling.

CLOSING AND PROTECTING THE BODY AGAINST UNEXPECTED ATTACKS

If you are attacked unexpectedly by a hail of incoming blows to your head, your instinctive reaction will be to protect yourself by raising your arms to your head. Krav maga builds on this natural reaction (see *Krav Maga*, page 9).

As strikes come to your head, pull your arms in from your regular outlet stance to form a defensive shield. Such a cover gives you a moment of protection as you regroup to escape or counterattack. To protect the head, bring both of your arms in front of your face with your forearms out to the side and your palm heels resting on the crown of your skull. The hand positioning is similar to your outlet stance; however, you are trying to seal any openings around your head. (Note: You can also use this "protect and cover" defense when on the ground.) After you regroup, burst forward with an attack of your own.

"LEG" DEFENSES AGAINST HOOK/ HAYMAKER PUNCHES

Krav maga, whenever possible, uses either a preemptive linear straight kick defense using the superior reach of the defender's legs or a deflection with a body defense to avoid an attack (including those with a weapon) and uses retzev counterattacks to neutralize the threat. While requiring advanced recognition and timing, a timing-defensive preemptive kick is extremely effective against hook/haymaker punch attacks. This technique will preempt your attacker before the attacker can land his punch. If I must fight, I will kick the attacker as soon as opportune, using fight timing.

INSTINCTIVE RETREAT COMBINED WITH A LEAD STRAIGHT KICK

From a passive stance, when something is launched at your head, you will instinctively throw a flinch response to defend, drawing your hands up to protect your head. This arm movement, in turn, helps pull your upper-body away from the incoming strike.

As you recognize the incoming strike (best done by observing the attacker's initial shoulder movement), take a step back with your right leg to facilitate the instinctive body defense rear lean as you rise on the ball of your left lead foot.

As you lean back to evade the hook/haymaker punch, use a timing-simultaneous straight lead leg kick against the attacker's groin. Launch the kick naturally by simply extending the leg forward using a natural trajectory. (Do not bring the knee up and then snap the kick out.) As always, keep your hands up; do not drop them. For maximum combative effect, be sure to pivot on the base of your right rear base leg to fully extend your left hip and drive your mass through the attacker. Follow up with additional combatives as necessary.

STRAIGHT LEAD LEG TIMING KICK AGAINST A RIGHT HOOK/HAYMAKER PUNCH

With enough distance and early recognition, you may use a lead straight timing kick to preempt or intercept an incoming hook punch before the attacker can reach you. Note that a looping hook or haymaker punch must travel slightly over three times as far to make contact compared to a linear strike. Importantly, this defense is conducted from a fighting stance where the defender clearly recognizes an attack is coming. Tactically, the defender has likely made up his mind to kick the attacker regardless of the method of the incoming attack.

From the left outlet stance resting on both balls of your feet, as the attacker launches the punch, use a front lead leg timing kick against the attacker's groin. Launch the kick by simply extending the leg forward using a natural trajectory. (Do not bring the knee up and then snap the kick out.) As always, keep your hands up; do not drop them. For maximum combative effect, be sure to pivot on the base of your rear right base to enable the full extension your left hip and drive your mass through the attacker. Follow up with additional combatives as necessary.

WHEN TO ASSUME A FIGHTING STANCE

If you assume a fighting stance, you must understand that the physical confrontation and ensuing violence may legally be considered one of mutual consent. In other words, it may be difficult for you to argue self-defense. Therefore the affirmative defense of self-defense may no longer be available. Conversely, if you inflict injury on your opponent, the opponent may have deemed to legally consent to the risk and consequences of fighting you. Nevertheless, your opponent could still take legal action against you for injuries sustained.

Tactically, however, if an opponent puts his hands up primed to injure you—your hands should come up into a fighting stance as you react. Notably, if you are extremely confident in your skill set, you may assume a low ready de-escalation stance or remain with your hands down. If you do not assume a defensive posture, certainly onlookers and possible video will portray you as less likely to be the aggressor.

Importantly, the reader will note that I only assume a fighting stance in five photo series (hook punch defenses using a straight kick and takedown defenses preventing a front tackle attempt) in chapters 4 and 9. All other tactics are performed from a low ready de-escalation position or a passive stance (where the defender is not anticipating an attack). The responsible citizen or kravist does not engage in fights and only physically reacts whenever all peaceful resolutions are exhausted.

STRAIGHT REAR LEG TIMING KICK AGAINST A RIGHT HOOK/HAYMAKER PUNCH

Again with enough distance and early recognition, you may use a rear straight timing kick to pre-empt or intercept an incoming hook punch before the attacker can reach you. Remember that a looping hook or haymaker punch must travel at least three times the distance to make contact. Note: The rear leg provides more power as you develop more torque by swinging the rear leg through but also requires exceptional timing and recognition. In other words, to use the rear leg, you must have enough distance and early recognition of an impending or incoming attack.

From the left outlet stance resting on both balls of your feet, as the attacker launches the punch, use a rear lead leg timing kick against the attacker's groin. Launch the kick by simply extending the leg forward using a natural trajectory. (Do not bring the knee up and then snap the kick out.) As always, keep your hands up; do not drop them.

For maximum combative effect, be sure to pivot on the base of your front left base leg to fully extend your left hip and drive your mass through the attacker. Follow up with additional combatives as necessary.

LEAD LEG TIMING SIDE KICK AGAINST A RIGHT HOOK/HAYMAKER PUNCH

You may also use a debilitating side kick to preempt an incoming hook punch before the attacker can reach you. Once again, a looping hook or haymaker punch must travel slightly over three times the distance compared to a linear strike. Importantly, the side kick is highly effective against any type of upper-body attack, particularly as the attacker is likely to load his weight on his front leg as the attacker tries to attack. This makes the damage you inflict that much more serious as you destroy the attacker's knee. Note: You must use your near-side front leg. (Trying to use your rear leg takes too much time as you must cross your body to bring the rear leg to bear.)

From the left outlet stance resting on both balls of your feet, as the attacker launches the punch, raise your front leg to prepare your side kick to the attacker's forward knee. Place your weight on the ball of the foot of your rear right foot. As always, keep your hands up; do not drop them.

For maximum combative effect, be sure to pivot on the base of your rear right base leg, with your toes pointed directly away from the attacker, to fully extend your left hip and drive your mass through the attacker's knee, while moving your upper body defensively away from the attacker. For an optimum side kick, be sure to deliver the impact with your heel. Follow up with additional combatives as necessary.

This drill requires two partners, P1 (the "Defender" [you]) and P2 ("Attacker" [your partner]). P1 faces P2 about one to three feet apart simulating a confrontation where P2 initiates as the aggressor. Practitioners should repeat this drill a minimum of 15 repetitions per kicking leg (30 repetitions total).

1. Against P2's hook/haymaker attempt, P1 delivers a straight front timing kick at 25% power—not full force—to the midsection (not the groin for safety purposes) of P2 to simulate stopping an advancing attacker (P2). P2 uses body absorption by tensing the midsection and abdominal muscles, while exhaling out strongly to create a vacuum when P1's ball of the foot makes contact. This drill may also be performed with a lead leg side kick.

2. Against P2's hook/haymaker attempt, P1 delivers a straight rear timing kick at 25% power—not full force—to the midsection (not the groin for safety purposes) of P2 to simulate stopping an advancing attacker (P2). P2 uses body absorption by tensing the midsection and abdominal muscles while exhaling out strongly to create a vacuum when P1's ball of the foot makes contact.

3. Both P1 and P2 have their hands down. P2 catches P1 in the "-5." Therefore, P1 must use a body retreat, rising on the ball of the front foot to pull the upper body away from the strike. As P1 retreats rearward to avoid P2's punch, P1 delivers a simulated straight kick to P2's groin.

4. This variation requires a suitable kicking pad or shield. Against P2's simulated push attempt (signaled by P2's movement toward P1), P1 delivers a straight front or straight rear timing kick using 50% power against a walk by P2, 75% power against a jog by P2, and 100% power against P2's run at P1. The pad holder, P2, should exhale on contact similar to step #1. This drill may also be performed with a lead leg side kick.

5. A variation of this drill may involve utilizing a hanging heavy bag, where P2 stands behind the bag and pushes the bag forward to simulate an attacker's advance. P1 delivers various levels of power with the rear kick variation to finish with retzev continuous combat motion. This drill may also be performed with a lead leg side kick.

6. As you improve your skill set and capabilities, you may then bolster your defense by adding two kicks or a kick and then knee combination.

    a. A straight kick and same-side straight punch or palm heel combination. In other words, if you kick with your right leg as soon as your foot makes contact with the target, initiate a straight punch or palm heel strike followed by additional punches, elbow strikes, knees, kicks, etc.

    b. Rear kick and turn into straight kick variation to finish with retzev continuous combat motion counterattacks.

Note: A variation of this drill can be used to defend against your partner attacking with straight punches, grabs, and chokes.

"HAND" DEFENSES AGAINST HOOK/HAY-MAKER PUNCHES

THE 360-DEGREE INSTINCTIVE DEFENSE AND COUNTERATTACK

Your instinctive 360-degree defenses counter outside attacks (such as slaps and roundhouse or hook punches), outside straight or sucker punches (whereby an assailant attempts to punch you in the face from an indirect off angle out of your line of vision), and knife or edged-weapon attacks.

From a de-escalatory stance (Note: Not a fighting stance, as you were attempting to reason with the aggressor), as you react to the incoming hook/haymaker punch, immediately begin to step off the line of attack while raising your arms up defensively. As you step off the line, simultaneously defend and attack by deflecting the incoming attacker's arm while punching the attacker's jaw, throat, nose, or eye socket.

As you deflect, be sure to bend your elbow approximately 70 degrees and rotate your arm outward 180 degrees to attack the attacker's arm. Essentially, you are performing a mini chop to the attacker's arm as you simultaneously strike the attacker in the face. Importantly, the deflection in itself is "attacking the attacker" by rotating your left deflecting arm, using a chopping motion to impact the attacker's incoming right arm.

A gunt variation may also be used while simultaneously counterattacking using anatomical targeting. From the left outlet stance, tuck your chin by burying it into your
right shoulder, while folding your arm across with your elbow tip pointed out on
approximately a 45-degree angle to intercept and block the hook punch at its earliest
stage and to act as a shock absorber. This avoids an indirect blow to your head
through your blocking arm's absorption of the strike. Do not fold the arm directly
against your head. Simultaneously attack the attacker's head or throat with a linear
counterstrike. This placement also sets up a convenient horizontal elbow counterattack
by then coming across with an elbow strike using the gunt arm to the attacker's neck
or head. You can also use the elbow tip after the block to draw it parallel to your head
and drive forward into the attacker's face.

Immediately transition from your counterpunch to deliver a combative forearm shiver to the side of the attacker's neck. This second counterattack is a dual-purpose combative in delivering a debilitating strike to the attacker's throat or carotid artery, while also setting you with a strong control position to deliver a knee to the attacker's groin. For maximum combative effect, be sure to pivot on the ball of your front base leg foot to fully extend your right hip and drive your mass through the attacker.

As you reduce the attacker's level through your knee to the groin strike, slip your left arm underneath the attacker's right arm to form a "V" clamp on the attacker's head by overlapping your palms to strongly secure the attacker's right arm against your shoulder.

Deliver a final knee to the attacker's head to ensure the attacker is no longer a physical threat to you. Once again, pivot correctly on the ball of the foot of your left leg for maximum combative effect. Finish with additional retzev combatives as necessary.

This drill requires two partners, P1 (the "Defender" [you]) and P2 ("Attacker" [your partner]). P1 faces P2 about one to three feet apart simulating a confrontation where P2 initiates as the aggressor. Practitioners should repeat this drill a minimum of 15 repetitions of right arm attacks and then left arm attacks (30 repetitions total).

1. Against P2's hook/haymaker attempt, P1 steps off the line of attack while forcefully rotating the left arm to the outside to deflect the incoming strike using a 360-degree outside rotational defense (attacking the attacker's arm) with P1's left arm while simultaneously counterattacking with P1's right arm, using a simulated straight punch or palm heel strike) close to P2's face without making contact.

2. As you improve your skill set and capabilities, repeat step #1 above but modify it by using an open-hand palm heel strike to make *light contact* against P2's head. Accordingly, in a variation of step #1 against P2's hook/haymaker attempt, P1 steps off the line of attack using a 360-degree outside rotational defense (attacking the attacker's arm) with a simulated open hand touch strike to P2's head to simulate stopping an advancing attacker. This crucial movement simulates both deflecting and attacking with both arms, underpinning krav maga's philosophy of simultaneous (or near simultaneous) defense and attack. As always, be careful not to injure your partner; but remember that in a real situation, you would use a close fist or palm heel strike targeting vulnerable areas. Of course, add additional combatives as you would like.

3. Reverse the above step using left attacks and the mirror-opposite defenses.

4. In a drill variation against P2's hook/haymaker attempt, P1 steps off the line of attack using an outside gunt defense (attacking the attacker's arm with the elbow tip) with a simulated open hand touch to P2's head to simulate stopping an advancing attacker. As always, be careful not to injure your partner; but remember in a real situation you would use a closed fist or palm heel strike targeting vulnerable areas. Of course, add additional combatives as you would like.

5. As you continue to improve your skill set and capabilities, you may then bolster your defense by adding:

    a. A straight left groin kick as you step off the line, loading your weight on your right stepping leg.

    b. Add two kicks or a kick and then knee combination.

    c. A nonstepping left groin kick to finish with retzev continuous combat motion counterattacks.

HOOK/HAYMAKER PUNCH DEFENSE WITH A STRAIGHT FOLLOW-UP KICK

This technique option demonstrates the continuous combat flow of krav maga by defending one of the most common attacks, a hook/haymaker punch.

From a passive stance, as soon as you recognize the attacker's shoulder movement signaling the incoming attack (primarily by watching the aggressor's shoulder movement), begin to step off the line of attack with your right leg, while immediately raising your arms into a defense and attack position.

As with the previous defense, simultaneously block and attack using a straight punch, web-of-the-hand strike to the throat, palm heel, or other option, targeting the attacker's vulnerable anatomy. By design, you have stepped of the line of attack, loading your weight onto your right leg. This weight lift facilitates a straight kick directly into the attacker's groin.

For maximum combative effect, be sure to pivot on the ball of the foot of your right base leg to fully extend your left hip, directing the groin kick through the attacker. Disengage or finish with additional retzev combatives as necessary.

HOOK/HAYMAKER PUNCH DOUBLE BLOCK WITH A STRAIGHT KNEE COUNTERATTACK

This defense builds on your instinctive flinch of bringing your arms up to protect your head and once again intercept an incoming threat or strike.

From a left outlet fighting stance, as you recognize the attacker's shoulder movement signaling the incoming attack, keep your elbows slightly bent beyond 90 degrees for maximum structural strength. Rotate your arms slightly outward to intercept the attacker's incoming arm with the fleshy undersides of your forearms.

Moving on the balls of your feet, burst forward into the attacker's arms with your forearms rigid. As you intercept the incoming hook/haymaker punch, accelerate your lower body forward and pivot on the ball of your left leg to ram your right knee through the attacker's groin. It is pivotal (forgive the pun) that you debilitate the attacker, as his left arm could deliver a strike. Depending on distance, you could also use a shin kick up through the attacker's groin. Continue with counterattacks such as a right forearm chop to the side of the attacker's neck combined with additional knee strikes and upper-body strikes as necessary to end the threat.

This alternative forearm interception block is similar to the previous defense except instead of using a straight knee strike substitute a roundhouse shin kick targeting the attacker's thigh. For maximum combative effect and to protect your base leg left knee, be sure to pivot on the ball of your left foot. Chop your shin through the attacker's left quadriceps muscle. Continue with counterattacks such as a right forearm chop to the side of the attacker's neck combined with additional knee strikes and upper-body strikes as necessary to end the threat.

HOOK/HAYMAKER PUNCH DOUBLE BLOCK DRILLS WITH A STRAIGHT KNEE COUNTERATTACK

This drill requires two partners, P1 (the "Defender" [you]) and P2 ("Attacker" [your partner]). P1 faces P2 about one to three feet apart simulating a confrontation where P2 initiates as the aggressor. Practitioners should repeat this drill a minimum of 15 repetitions of right arm attacks and then left arm attacks (30 repetitions total).

1. Against P2's hook/haymaker attempt, P1 raises both arms (bent with elbows beyond 90 degrees) to burst into P2's incoming arm by stepping with the P1's left leg. As P1 steps into P2, transferring all of P1's body weight against P2's arm, P1 delivers a simultaneous simulated straight knee strike into P2's groin, thigh, or midsection.

2. Reverse the above step using left attacks.

3. As you continue to improve your skill set and capabilities, you may then bolster your defense by adding a follow-up chop with your right arm followed by additional knee strikes into retzev continuous combat motion counterattacks.

HOOK/HAYMAKER PUNCH DOUBLE BLOCK
WITH A CHOP COUNTERATTACK

This technique demonstrates once again the instinctive nature of krav maga by harnessing one's natural response of flinching or placing two arms up to shield the upper body. The only drawback to this defense is if the attacker launches a right hook and immediately launches a left punch as you have committed two hands to defending the right hook. By committing two hands, you have left your right side open to the attacker's left arm delivering a strike.

Defending from an interview/de-escalation or when caught in the "-5." Simultaneously intercept the punch with both arms, using an approximate 60-degree bend, making contact with the underside of your arms (ulnar bones) against the assailant's incoming strike.

Immediately use a chop to the carotid sheath. Follow-up with additional combatives, including a straight knee to the thigh or, if necessary, to the groin.

HOOK/HAYMAKER PUNCH DOUBLE BLOCK DRILLS WITH A CHOP COUNTERATTACK

This drill requires two partners, P1 (the "Defender" [you]) and P2 ("Attacker" [your partner]). P1 faces P2 about one to three feet apart simulating a confrontation where P2 initiates as the aggressor. Practitioners should repeat this drill a minimum of 15 repetitions of right-arm attacks and then left-arm attacks (30 repetitions total).

1. Against P2's hook/haymaker attempt, P1 raises both arms (bent with elbows beyond 90 degrees for extensor strength) to burst into P2's incoming arm by stepping with the P1's left leg. P1 bursts into P2 using a left diagonal step thereby transferring all of P1's body mass against the hook/haymaker attack. This tactical movement allows P1 to immediately deliver a simulated outside chop to the carotid sinus of P2's neck followed by a straight right knee counterattack followed by retzev. Be careful about making contact to P2's neck.

2. Reverse the above step using left attacks.

HOOK/HAYMAKER PUNCH DEFENSE USING OUTSIDE 360-DEGREE DEFENSE WHILE TEXTING

A favored ambush tactic is to attack a victim target who is distracted. Texting creates vulnerabilities as the intended victim will have his head down and hands occupied. React to this attack using the same instinctive tactics you already know, while taking advantage that your hands are partially raised.

As you recognize the incoming hook/haymaker punch, immediately begin to step off the line of attack, while instinctively raising your arms up defensively. As you step off the line, simultaneously defend and attack by deflecting the incoming attacker's arm, while using your device to strike the attacker in the jaw, throat, nose, or eye socket. Note: You may drop your device as you step off the line and use a hand strike instead; however, a mobile device can be a highly effective weapon of opportunity.

As you deflect, be sure to bend your elbow approximately 70 degrees and rotate the outward deflecting arm 180 degrees to attack the attacker's arm. Once again, you are performing a mini chop to the attacker's arm as you strike the attacker in the face or throat.

By design, you have stepped off the line of attack, loading your weight onto your right leg. As a follow-up combative (see photos on page 97) this weight shift facilitates a straight kick directly into the attacker's groin. For maximum combative effect, be sure to pivot on the foot of your right base leg to fully extend your left hip, directing the groin kick through the attacker. Finish with retzev combatives as necessary.

This drill requires two partners, P1 (the "Defender" [you]) and P2 ("Attacker" [your partner]). P1 faces P2 about one to three feet apart simulating a confrontation where P2 initiates as the aggressor. Practitioners should repeat this drill a minimum of 15 repetitions of right arm attacks and then left arm attacks (30 repetitions total).

1. Against P2's hook/haymaker attempt, P1 steps off the line of attack, while forcefully rotating the left arm to the outside to deflect the incoming strike with P1's left arm, while simultaneously counterattacking using P1's right arm holding the device as a weapon of opportunity, striking close to P2's face without making contact.

2. Reverse the above step using left attacks.

3. As you continue to improve your skill set and capabilities, you may then bolster your defense by adding:

   a. A straight left kick as you step off the line, loading your weight on your right stepping leg.

   b. Add two kicks or a kick and then knee combination.

   c. A nonstepping leg kick to finish with retzev continuous combat motion counterattacks.

Using your peripheral vision, as soon as you recognize the incoming hook/haymaker strike, take advantage of your partially raised hands to intercept the attacker's arm.

To intercept the attacker's incoming arm, immediately raise both of your arms (building on an instinctive flinch mechanism), while bending your elbows slightly beyond 90 degrees for maximum structural strength. Rotate your arms slightly outward to intercept the attacker's incoming arm with the underside (ulna bone) of your forearms. Immediately transition from your double-arm interception tactic into a chop to the attacker's neck, using your near-side right arm. Once again, debilitate him quickly, because the left arm poses a danger.

Follow up with a right shin kick to the attacker's groin followed by additional retzev combatives as necessary.

HOOK/HAYMAKER PUNCH DEFENSE FROM THE SIDE WHILE TEXTING

This drill requires two partners, P1 (the "Defender" [you]) and P2 ("Attacker" [your partner]). P1 faces P2 about one to three feet apart simulating a confrontation where P2 initiates as the aggressor. P1 should have a mock phone or object to simulate texting. Practitioners should repeat this drill a minimum of 15 repetitions of right arm attacks and then left arm attacks (30 repetitions total).

1. Against P2's straight sucker punch attempt, P1 steps off the line of attack with the outside right leg away from the right incoming punch while simultaneously raising both arms to instinctively intercept the punching arm with the underside of his forearms. Immediately simulate a counter-attack with a forearm strike to the neck followed by the additional combatives.

2. Reverse the above step using left attacks.

3. As you continue to improve your skill set and capabilities, finish with retzev continuous combat motion counterattacks.

FIVE

STRAIGHT PUNCH DEFENSES

KRAV MAGA, YET AGAIN, WHENEVER POSSIBLE, USES EITHER A PREEMPTORY

KICK DEFENSE USING THE SUPERIOR REACH OF THE DEFENDER'S LEGS OR A

DEFLECTION WITH A BODY DEFENSE TO AVOID AN ATTACK (INCLUDING THOSE WITH

A WEAPON) AND USES RETZEV COUNTERATTACKS TO NEUTRALIZE THE THREAT.

TIMING KICK DEFENSES AGAINST PUNCHES

While requiring advanced recognition and timing, a timing-defensive linear straight kick can also be extremely effective against linear punch attacks. This technique will preempt your attacker before the attacker can land his punch. Note: Keeping in line with krav maga tactical and strategic thinking, these timing defenses are almost identical to the straight push defenses using both lead and rear leg timing kicks you learned in chapter 2.

As you recognize the attacker begin to coil his shoulder, and step toward you, begin to pivot on the ball of the foot of your rear (right) leg. This begins to transfer your weight forward as you extend your forward (left) leg through the attacker's groin. Note: This pivot is already primed and in place as you stand in your low ready de-escalation position with your weight placed on both balls of your feet. As you deliver the straight kick, launch your left leg forward naturally as you would kick a bouncing ball. Do not pull your knee up abnormally and then thrust your leg out. Be sure to raise your arms

up as this helps pull your body weight forward while also placing you in a proper fighting stance to continue your counterattack as needed. Curl you toes and kick with the ball of your foot. Kick your attacker in the knee, groin, or midsection as the attacker tries to deliver a straight punch (or any other type of upper-body attack.) Follow up with additional retzev counterattacks as necessary. Importantly, you could also use your rear right leg, provided you recognized the incoming attack in time to launch the rear kick (similar to timing kick defense against a hook punch defense found on pages 82–85).

This drill requires two partners, P1 (the "Defender" [you]) and P2 ("Attacker" [your partner]). P1 faces P2 simulating about three to six feet apart in a simulated confrontation where P2 initiates as the aggressor. Practitioners should repeat this drill a minimum of 15 repetitions per kicking leg (30 repetitions total).

1. Against P2's straight punch attempt, P1 delivers straight front and rear straight timing kicks at 25% power—not full force—to the midsection (not the groin for safety purposes) of P2 to simulate stopping an advancing attacker (P2). These are light kicks. P2 uses body absorption by tensing the midsection and abdominal muscles, while exhaling out strongly to create a vacuum when the ball of P1's foot makes contact.

2. This variation requires a suitable kicking pad or shield. Against P2's simulated straight punch attempt that can be signaled by P2 using a stomp (enabling P2 to hold the pad firmly), P1 delivers straight front straight timing kicks using 25%, 50%, and 100% power and explosion. The pad holder, P2, should exhale on contact similar to step #1. Note: A hanging heavy bag may be substituted where P2 stands behind the bag and pushes the bag forward to simulate an attacker initiating a punch. P1 delivers various levels of power, as noted above.

3. In a variation of this drill, a hanging heavy bag may be substituted where P2 stands behind the bag and pushes the bag forward to simulate an attacker initiating a punch. P1 delivers various levels of power, as noted above.

4. As you improve your skill set and capabilities, you may then bolster your defense by adding:

   a. Two kicks or a kick and then knee combination.

   b. A straight kick and same-side straight punch or palm heel combination. In other words, if you kick with your right leg as soon as your foot makes contact with the target, initiate a straight punch or palm heel strike followed by additional punches, elbow strikes, knees, kicks, etc.

   c. Rear kick and turn into straight kick variation to finish with retzev continuous combat motion counterattacks.

Note: A variation of this drill can be used to defend against your partner attacking with straight punches, grabs, and chokes.

INSIDE OVER-THE-TOP SLIDING PARRY AGAINST A STRAIGHT FRONT PUNCH WHILE STEPPING OFF THE LINE

This defense allows you deflect an incoming punch from either side while simultaneously moving away from the punch and delivering your own straight punch counterattack to the throat, chin, or temple. The intercepting arm should always lead the body, or the arm deflection should precede by fractions of a second the body's defensive movement. This gets you out of the line of fire or "off the line" to provide a double layer of protection, redirecting a threat while at the same moment moving yourself away from the threat.

From your low ready de-escalation stance, as the straight punch comes in, initiate with your left leg to step slightly to your left off the line of attack while bringing your right leg with you. Move (and remain) on the balls of both your feet. Simultaneously deflect and drive the attacker's arm downward by using an inverted punch (pinkie down, thumb up). Be sure to extend your body reach to its fullest by pivoting toward your target on the same-side leg as your deflecting arm. Keep your chin tucked and buried into your shoulder. Continue with counterattacks such as a rear knee to the attacker's groin, thigh, or midsection, followed by additional knee strikes and upper-body strikes as necessary to end the threat.

INSIDE OVER-THE-TOP SLIDING PARRY AGAINST A STRAIGHT FRONT PUNCH WHILE STEPPING OFF-THE-LINE DRILLS

This drill requires two partners, P1 (the "Defender" [you]) and P2 ("Attacker" [your partner]). P1 faces P2 about one to three feet apart simulating a confrontation where P2 initiates as the aggressor. Practitioners should repeat this drill a minimum of 15 repetitions with each outlet stance (30 repetitions total).

1. Against P2's straight right punch attempt, P1 steps slightly off the line of attack while intercepting P2's right arm with P1's left (counterpunching) arm. P1 uses an inverted punch to force P2's arm down, while P1 slides the simulated over-the-top punch to simulate striking P2 in the temple, ear, or jaw. Follow up with retzev counterattacks.

2. This drill should be repeated with P1 in a right outlet stance and P2 in a left outlet stance.

3. This drill should be repeated with P1 in a left outlet stance and P2 in a right outlet stance.

Note: A variation of this drill can be used to defend against your partner attacking with grabs and chokes.

INSIDE SLIDING PARRY AGAINST A STRAIGHT REAR PUNCH WHILE STEPPING OFF THE LINE

From a passive stance, as you recognize the attacker begin to move toward you or to step and coil his shoulder, initiate with your left leg to step slightly off the line of attack to your left while bringing your right leg with you. Move (and remain) on the balls of both of your feet. Against a right punch, as you step to your left, simultaneously bring your left hand cupped diagonally across your face close to your left shoulder to deflect the incoming punch.

Your left hand will deflect the incoming punch, sliding up the attacker's arm. Be sure to move "deep" into the attacker and not leave your deflecting arm behind you. Remember, the attacker is likely to retract his punching arm. With your right arm, simultaneously deliver a half-hook counterpunch to your attacker's throat, chin, or nose. You will achieve advantageous dead-side positioning. The key, again, is to deflect and step off the line and moving both feet together. Do not lunge; keep your feet equidistant by moving them the same distance.

This defense is readily followed up with trapping the attacker's left arm and delivering a left straight knee to the groin or midsection, followed by a right over-the-top-elbow (using just below your elbow tip) to the back of the attacker's head or neck. Be sure to pivot your base leg and transfer your weight properly for additional counterattacks. Additional retzev combatives should follow. A follow-up choke option from this technique is a standing triangle choke (not depicted). Lastly, a number of strong takedowns are available, including multiple takedown options to land an attacker hard on his head or to create a standing triangular choke position that also involves taking the attacker down into formidable choke positions on the ground.

Note: For both inside sliding parry defenses, if you misread the assailant's straight punch (i.e., the attacker throws a right instead of a left), stepping off the line properly will still allow the defense to work. Effectively, you will have avoided the punch with a body defense (stepping off the line of attack) while counterattacking. In essence, you will "split" the attacker's hands with your counterpunch. The immediate danger is if you are still positioned to your attacker's live side, because the attacker may still have the ability to mount an effective counterattack. The preferred defense is always to move to the attacker's dead side, minimizing the attacker's ability to counterattack. Your counterpunch is easily followed up by a right rear straight kick, as you have transferred your weight to your left leg.

Note also that the inside sliding parry defenses can be used when on the ground. The key is a strong body defense while moving away to the dead side to the punch with a proper slide and simultaneous counterpunch. Be sure to slide fully up the arm as you simultaneously counterpunch to set up additional combatives including, but not limited to, a short palm heel strike to the head or throat to position you on your side for a straight arm bar.

INSIDE SLIDING PARRY AGAINST A STRAIGHT REAR PUNCH WHILE STEPPING OFF-THE-LINE DRILLS

This drill requires two partners, P1 (the "Defender" [you]) and P2 ("Attacker" [your partner]). P1 faces P2 about one to three feet apart simulating a confrontation where P2 initiates as the aggressor. Practitioners should repeat this drill a minimum of 15 repetitions from each of the left and right outlet stances (30 repetitions total).

1. Against P2's straight right punch attempt, P1 steps slightly off the line of attack while intercepting P2's right arm with P1's left arm. As P1 intercepts and parries while sliding up P2's incoming arm, P1 simultaneously simulates a counterpunch with P1's right arm. P1 may use a strong follow-up right straight knee to P2's groin, thigh, or midsection. Follow up with retzev counterattacks.

2. This drill should be repeated with P1 in a right outlet stance and P2 in a left outlet stance.

3. This drill should be repeated with P1 in a left outlet stance and P2 in a right outlet stance.

SUCKER PUNCH DEFENSE WHILE TEXTING: MODIFIED INSIDE SLIDING PARRY AGAINST A STRAIGHT REAR PUNCH WHILE STEPPING OFF THE LINE

From a passive stance while texting, identical to the previous defense, as you recognize the attacker begin to step and coil his shoulder, initiating with your left leg, step slightly off the line of attack to your left, while bringing your right leg with you. Move (and remain) on the balls of both of your feet. Against a right punch, as you step to your left, simultaneously bring your left hand cupped diagonally across your face close to your left shoulder.

Your left hand will deflect the incoming punch and slide high up the attacker's arm. With your right arm, use your device as a weapon of opportunity to counterattack your attacker's throat, chin, or nose. You will achieve dead-side positioning. The key, again, is to deflect and step off the line deep to the deadside while moving both feet together. Do not lunge; keep your feet equidistant by moving them the same distance. This defense, once again, similar to the previous defense, is readily followed up with trapping the attacker's left arm and delivering a left straight knee to the groin or midsection, followed by a right over-the-top-elbow (using just below your elbow tip) to the back of the attacker's head or neck. Be sure to pivot your base leg and transfer your weight properly for additional counterattacks. Additional debilitating retzev combatives should follow.

SUCKER PUNCH DEFENSE WHILE TEXTING: MODIFIED INSIDE SLIDING PARRY AGAINST A STRAIGHT REAR PUNCH WHILE STEPPING OFF-THE-LINE DRILLS

This drill requires two partners, P1 (the "Defender" [you]) and P2 ("Attacker" [your partner]). P1 faces P2 about one to three feet apart simulating a confrontation where P2 initiates as the aggressor. P1 should hold a mock phone or other object to simulate texting (being distracted.) Practitioners should repeat this drill a minimum of 15 repetitions for each of the left and right outlet stances (30 repetitions total).

1. Against P2's straight right punch attempt, P1 steps slightly off the line of attack, while intercepting P2's right arm with P1's left arm. As P1 intercepts and parries by sliding up P2's incoming arm, P1 simultaneously simulates a strike with the device held in P1's right arm. P1 may use a strong follow-up right straight knee to P2's groin, thigh, or midsection. Follow up with retzev counterattacks.

2. This drill should be repeated with P1 in a right outlet stance and P2 in a left outlet stance.

3. This drill should be repeated with P1 in a left outlet stance and P2 in a right outlet stance.

TIMING SIDE KICK AGAINST A SUCKER PUNCH

This instinctive defense allows you to duck your head into your shoulder while moving your torso away to protect your head. This kick allows for a formidable simultaneous defense and attack option—krav maga's fundamental tenet for stopping an attacker.

As you recognize the incoming attack, use a simultaneous side kick to the assailant's knee. Pick up your near-side right leg and deliver a devastating side kick with proper base-leg movement by pivoting on the ball of the foot to direct your base-leg heel toward your attacker for maximum power and reach. Importantly, this defense also works against an attacker standing to your side, but facing in the opposite direction. It is also effective against an attacker standing in the same direction.

Note: The inside sliding parry defenses previously introduced may work against this type of attack; however, timing—as with all defenses—is crucial. You must step out of the line of attack in time to deflect and counterpunch.

OUTSIDE DEFLECTION DEFENSE AGAINST A STRAIGHT SUCKER PUNCH USING A SIDE KICK

Once again, a sucker punch blindsiding of a victim is a favored ambush tactic. To defend, obviously you must recognize the incoming attack using your peripheral vision. This technique deflects a straight punch delivered by an attacker standing to your side.

From a passive stance, as you recognize the attacker begin to step and coil his shoulder or move toward you, initiate the defense with your left leg by stepping slightly off the line of attack to your left. As you step with your left leg, bring your right leg with you and move (and remain) on both balls of your feet. As you step off the line of attack, use an outside rotational block or 360-degree instinctive defense to intercept and deflect the incoming punch. As you deflect, be sure to bend your elbow approximately 70 degrees and rotate your arm outward 108 degrees to attack the attacker's arm. Again, you are attacking the attacker's arm with the modified 360-degree defense mini chop.

As you step off the line of attack to deflect the incoming punch, your left step loads your weight on your left leg. Place your weight on the ball of your left foot. This allows your right leg to deliver a devastating side kick to the attacker's near-side knee. Remember, the attacker has likely loaded his weight on this leg, making the damage you will inflict that much worse.

To deliver the side kick, pick up your near-side right leg. With proper left base-leg movement, pivot on the ball of the foot to direct your base-leg heel toward your attacker. This creates maximum power and reach to deliver a devastating side kick. As you deliver the right side kick, pivot on the ball of the foot of your left leg. Drive your right heel through the attacker's knee. For maximum combative effect, be sure to pivot on the base of your left right base leg with your toes pointed directly away from the attacker to fully extend your left hip and drive your mass through the attacker's knee. For an optimum side kick, be sure to deliver the impact with your heel. As always, keep your hands up; do not drop them. Follow up with additional combatives as necessary or disengage moving to safety.

OUTSIDE DEFENSE AGAINST A STRAIGHT SUCKER PUNCH USING A TIMING SIDE KICK

This drill requires two partners, P1 (the "Defender" [you]) and P2 ("Attacker" [your partner]). P1 faces P2 about one to three feet apart simulating a confrontation where P2 initiates as the aggressor. P1 and P2 are facing in opposite directions. Practitioners should repeat this drill a minimum of 15 repetitions per kicking leg (30 repetitions total).

1. Against P2's straight punch attempt, P1 delivers a simulated properly executed side kick with the near-side leg to P2's knee. Be careful not to injure P2's knee.

2. A variation requires a suitable kicking pad or shield. Against P2's simulated straight punch attempt that can be signaled by P2 using a stomp (enabling P2 to hold the pad firmly), P1 delivers a near-side timing side kick using 25%, 50%, and 100% power and explosion. The pad holder, P2, should exhale on contact similar to step #1.

3. A variation of this drill may use a hanging heavy bag where P2 stands behind the bag and pushes the bag forward to simulate an attacker initiating a punch. P1 delivers various levels of power as noted above.

OUTSIDE DEFLECTION DEFENSE AGAINST A STRAIGHT SUCKER PUNCH USING COUNTERPUNCHES

Similar to the previous defense, you may also step off the line of attack and counterattack, using upper-body strikes such as body hook punches or chops to the kidneys followed by additional retzev combatives. Note: In this defense the attacker is facing the opposite direction.

From a passive stance, as you recognize the attacker begin to step and coil his shoulder, initiate with your left leg to step slightly off the line of attack to your left. As you step with your left leg, bring your right leg with you. Move (and remain) on the balls of both of your feet. As you step off the line of attack, use an outside rotational block or 360-degree instinctive defense to intercept and deflect the incoming punch. As you deflect, be sure to bend your elbow approximately 70 degrees and rotate your arm outward 108 degrees to attack the attacker's arm. Again, you are attacking the attacker's arm with the modified 360-degree defense mini chop. Your left step loads your weight on your left leg.

Transfer your weight to the ball of your left foot. This allows you to pivot strongly into your preferred counterattack with maximum power, including the kidney counterpunch, as depicted.

OUTSIDE DEFENSE AGAINST A STRAIGHT SUCKER PUNCH USING THE SAME ARM TO DEFLECT AND COUNTERSTRIKE DRILLS

This drill requires two partners, P1 (the "Defender" [you]) and P2 ("Attacker" [your partner]). P1 and P2 should stand about three feet apart from one another while facing in the opposite directions. Practitioners should repeat this drill a minimum of 15 repetitions of both right arm attacks and then left arm attacks (30 repetitions total).

1. Against P2's straight sucker punch attempt, P1 steps off the line of attack with the outside left leg, while forcefully rotating the right arm to the outside to deflect the incoming strike. By stepping with outside left leg, P1 has loaded the weight on the left leg to pivot on the ball of the foot and deliver a simulated body punch or chop against P2's kidneys.

2. Reverse the above drill, using right-handed straight punch attacks.

3. As you continue to improve your skill set and capabilities, finish with retzev continuous combat motion counterattacks.

OUTSIDE DEFLECTION DEFENSE AGAINST A STRAIGHT SUCKER PUNCH USING THE SAME ARM TO DEFLECT AND COUNTERSTRIKE

Similar to the previous defense, you may also step off the line of attack and counterattack using the same arm followed, if necessary, by additional retzev combatives. Note: In this defense, the attacker is facing the same direction.

From a passive stance, as you recognize the attacker begin to step and coil his shoulder, initiate with your left leg to step slightly off the line of attack to your left while bringing your right leg with you. Move (and remain) on the balls of both of your feet. As you step off the line of attack, use an outside rotational block or 360-degree instinctive defense to intercept and deflect the incoming punch. As you deflect, be sure to bend your elbow approximately 70 degrees and rotate your arm outward 108 degrees to attack the attacker's arm. Again, you are attacking the attacker's arm with the modified 360-degree defense mini chop.

As soon as you deflect the incoming strike, immediately counterattack using either a forefinger and middle finger knuckle strike to the attacker's temple or a palm heel strike to the attacker's ear. Follow up with additional retzev combatives as needed.

OUTSIDE DEFENSE AGAINST A STRAIGHT SUCKER PUNCH USING THE SAME ARM TO DEFLECT AND COUNTERSTRIKE DRILLS

This drill requires two partners, P1 (the "Defender" [you]) and P2 ("Attacker" [your partner]). P1 faces P2 about one to three feet, facing in the same direction where P2 initiates as the aggressor. Practitioners should repeat this drill a minimum of 15 repetitions of right arm attacks and then left arm attacks (30 repetitions total).

1. Against P2's straight sucker punch attempt, P1 steps off the line of attack with the outside right leg, while forcefully rotating the right arm to the outside (mini outside chop) to deflect the incoming strike. By stepping with outside leg, P1 has loaded the weight on the right leg. P1 delivers either a simulated knuckle strike to P2's temple or palm heel combative to P2's ear or jaw. As you continue to improve your skill set and capabilities, finish with retzev continuous combat motion counterattacks.

2. Reverse the above drill using left attacks.

SIX

DEFENDING AGAINST STRAIGHT KICKS AND KNEES

YOUR REGULAR OUTLET STANCE ALLOWS YOU TO DEFEND A MYRIAD OF ATTACKS

WITHOUT COMPROMISING YOUR ABILITY TO DEFEND OTHER PARTS OF YOUR BODY

SHOULD THEY BE ATTACKED SIMULTANEOUSLY. THESE DEFENSES ARE DESIGNED

TO COUNTER STRAIGHT KICKS LAUNCHED AGAINST YOU. OPTIMALLY, USE YOUR front leg to parry the kick, but, occasionally, a hand defense may be necessary. Remember that lowering your hands to defend against a kick can expose you to upper-body strikes, particularly straight punches, so be careful when defending kicks with your arms.

Contemplate your response if someone were to kick at your groin. You'd probably drop your hands and contort your body, bringing one leg across the other to protect your groin. Krav maga builds on this response but modifies your action. For this particular defense do not drop your hands because this will leave your face open to attack. In the following pages you'll learn how to use your natural instincts to defend against groin kicks and other incoming attacks.

THE SHIN DEFLECTION AGAINST A STRAIGHT KICK

The shin deflection defends against a low straight kick regardless of which leg the attacker uses.

From your regular outlet stance, use your front leg or foot to deflect or parry an incoming kick without dropping your hands. Slide your front leg across your body while maintaining your balance, but do not overcommit your front leg, which may throw you off balance, and, more important, put you in a vulnerable position.

Once you successfully parry the kick, transition immediately back into your regular outlet stance by simultaneously delivering a strong straight punch to the attacker's head, using the first two knuckles of your forefinger and middle fingers. Optimally, deliver the strike as your left foot touches down to transfer all of your body weight through the strike. Follow up with additional retzev combatives as necessary—such as a shin kick to the attacker's groin.

THE SHIN DEFLECTION AGAINST A STRAIGHT KICK

This drill requires two partners, P1 (the "Defender" [you]) and P2 ("Attacker" [your partner]). P1 faces P2 about three to six feet apart simulating a confrontation where P2 initiates as the aggressor. Suitable martial arts–style shin guards may be used. Practitioners should repeat this drill a minimum of 15 repetitions for both front and rear leg straight kicks (30 repetitions total).

1. Against P2's straight front or rear leg kick attempt, P1 deflects P2's incoming straight kick and counterattacks using upper-body combatives (combined with lower-body combatives). As you continue to improve your skill set and capabilities, finish with immediate retzev continuous combat motion counterattacks.

2. Reverse the above drill using an opposite outlet stance.

INTERCEPTING SIDE KICK

This defense (not depicted) against a low straight kick requires a great amount of timing to intercept the kick with your foot. From your regular outlet stance, raise your front leg and turn your foot parallel to the ground, using your foot's entire length to intercept your attacker's kicking foot before it has a chance to fully launch (see *Krav Maga: An Essential Guide,* page 97).

BODY DEFENSE AND UPPER-BODY COUNTERATTACK AGAINST A STRAIGHT KICK BY MOVING OFF THE LINE

This sidestep timing body defense takes you off the line of fire and uses a counterpunch to stun the attacker.

From the left outlet stance, take a body defense sidestep to your left to avoid the straight kick. As you step, simultaneously deliver a strong right counterpunch to the attacker's neck, jaw, or nose, followed by retzev combatives.

BODY DEFENSE AND UPPER-BODY COUNTERATTACK AGAINST A STRAIGHT KICK BY MOVING OFF THE LINE

This drill requires two partners, P1 (the "Defender" [you]) and P2 ("Attacker" [your partner]). P1 faces P2 about three to six feet apart simulating a confrontation where P2 initiates as the aggressor. P1 and P2 are facing in the same direction. Practitioners should repeat this drill a minimum of 15 repetitions for both front and rear leg straight kicks (30 repetitions total).

1. Against P2's straight front or rear leg kick attempt, P1 steps off the line of attack while simultaneously delivering a straight lead punch or palm heel to P2's head. As you continue to improve your skill set and capabilities, finish with immediate retzev continuous combat motion counterattacks.

2. Reverse the above drill using an opposite outlet stance.

KNEE DEFLECTION AGAINST A STRAIGHT KNEE TO THE GROIN

The knee deflection defends against a low straight knee to the groin regardless of which leg the attacker uses.

From a passive stance, use your left leg to deflect or parry an incoming groin-level straight knee. As you deflect, bring your hands up to both defend and counterattack. Be sure to parry the incoming knee enough to send it off course, but not so much as to turn your entire body around. In other words, slide your front leg across your body while maintaining your balance but do not overcommit your front leg, which may throw you off balance, and, more important, put you in a vulnerable position.

Once you successfully parry the knee strike, transition immediately into your regular outlet stance by simultaneously delivering an eye gouge or strong straight punch to the attacker's head. Optimally, deliver the eye strike as your left foot touches down.

Follow up with a chop to attacker's neck, accompanied by additional retzev combatives as necessary.

KNEE DEFLECTION AGAINST A STRAIGHT KNEE TO THE GROIN

This drill requires two partners, P1 (the "Defender" [you]) and P2 ("Attacker" [your partner]). P1 faces P2 about one to three feet apart simulating a confrontation where P2 initiates as the aggressor. P1 and P2 are facing in the same direction. Practitioners should repeat this drill a minimum of 15 repetitions for both front and rear leg straight kicks (30 repetitions total).

1. Against P2's straight front or rear knee kick attempt, P1 deflects P2's incoming straight knee with P1's preferred leg and counterattacks, using upper-body combatives (combined with lower-body combatives). As you continue to improve your skill set and capabilities, finish with immediate retzev continuous combat motion counterattacks.

2. Reverse the above drill using an opposite outlet stance.

HAND DEFLECTION AGAINST A STRAIGHT KNEE TO THE GROIN

The knee deflection defends against a low straight knee to the groin regardless of which leg the attacker uses.

From a passive stance, as you recognize the incoming knee, step slightly to your left, off the line of attack, while simultaneously using your left hand to deflect or parry an incoming groin-level straight knee.

As you deflect and simultaneously step off the line of attack, be sure to keep a slight bend in your left elbow to avoid hyperextending it, while also bringing your right hand up to both defend and counterattack as necessary. Deliver a strong straight punch to the attacker's head, making sure to use correct wrist alignment, weight transfer, and targeting accompanied by additional retzev combatives as necessary.

HAND DEFLECTION AGAINST A STRAIGHT KNEE TO THE GROIN DRILL

This drill requires two partners, P1 (the "Defender" [you]) and P2 ("Attacker" [your partner]). P1 faces P2 about one foot apart simulating a confrontation where P2 initiates as the aggressor. Practitioners should repeat this drill a minimum of 15 repetitions for both front and rear leg straight kicks (30 repetitions total).

1. Against P2's straight front or rear knee kick attempt, P1 deflects P2's incoming straight knee with P1's same-side arm (making sure to keep the elbow slightly bent to prevent hyper-extension) while stepping off the line of attack. P1 immediately simulates a side kick to P2 with P1's preferred leg and counterattacks using upper-body combatives (combined with lower-body combatives). As you continue to improve your skill set and capabilities, finish with immediate retzev continuous combat motion counterattacks.

2. Reverse the above drill using an opposite outlet stance.

One of the most dangerous positions is to find yourself on the ground with an attacker hovering over you prepared to stomp your head or some other vulnerable part of your anatomy. Of course, you should try to preempt any type of attack by kicking out the attacker's knees or ankles. The attacker can generate tremendous force, combining his leg strength, weight, and gravity to seriously injure you. You must try position yourself away from an attacker's legs. To defend against a straight stomp to the head, use a combined 360-degree outside defense and body defense to deflect the incoming kick.

With you near-side leg raised in a defensive posture, you may wish to clench your fist to strengthen your deflecting arm as you rotate it to the outside. As you rotate the arm outward, simultaneously use a body defense snake movement to maneuver your body off the line of attack and away from the kick.

Note: If the attacker were closer to your lower body, you could use your near-side leg to intercept and deflect the kick away; however, most attackers will naturally target your head, necessitating an upper-body arm-deflection defense.

Moving off the line of attack has necessarily repositioned your body. As you reposition, continue to turn onto your left hip to use your own side kick to the attacker's most proximate knee. Get up immediately to escape or close on the felled attacker with strong kicks of your own to end the threat.

OUTSIDE DEFENSE AGAINST A STRAIGHT SUCKER PUNCH USING THE SAME ARM TO DEFLECT AND COUNTERSTRIKE DRILLS

This drill requires two partners, P1 (the "Defender" [you]) and P2 ("Attacker" [your partner]). P1 faces P2 about one to three feet apart simulating a confrontation where P2 initiates as the aggressor. P1 is on P1's back while P2 is standing near P1's side facing P1. Practitioners should repeat this drill a minimum of 15 repetitions for both right and left kick attacks (30 repetitions total).

1. Against P2's right straight stomp attempt, P1 shimmies off the line of attack, while forcefully rotating the right arm (a mini outside chop recommended, with a clenched fist) to the outside to deflect the incoming kick. As P1 deflects P2's kick, P2's momentum will shift. P1 uses the body shimmy defense to position P1 to deliver a simulated side kick to P2's knee.

2. Reverse the above drill using a left kick (P2 is positioned to P1's left side).

ROUNDHOUSE KICK DEFENSE WHILE ON THE GROUND

Again, one of the most dangerous positions is to find yourself on the ground with an attacker hovering over you prepared to deliver a kick to your head. As noted, you should try to preempt any type of attack by kicking out the attacker's knees or ankles. The attacker can generate tremendous force by combining leg strength, weight, and gravity to seriously injure you. To defend against a soccer-style kick to the head, use a combined outside upper-body gunt and lower-body leg defense to intercept and thwart the incoming kick.

To defend against a roundhouse kick to the head, employ an angled gunt, using the tip of your elbow against the attacker's shin, combined with a lower-body leg shield, by raising your knee to your chest. Prepare immediately to launch a straight heel kick into the attacker's exposed groin with your heel.

Using your deflecting leg, employing krav maga economy of motion, kick the attacker in the attacker's groin with the attacker's heel.

ROUNDHOUSE KICK DEFENSE WHILE ON THE GROUND DRILLS

This drill requires two partners, P1 (the "Defender" [you]) and P2 ("Attacker" [your partner]). P1 faces P2 simulating a confrontation where P2 initiates as the aggressor. P2 is within kicking range of P1's head. P1 is on P1's back, while P2 is standing near P1's side facing P1. Practitioners should repeat this drill a minimum of 15 repetitions for both right and left kick attacks (30 repetitions total).

1. Against P2's left roundhouse kick attempt, P1 raises P1's same-side leg, pulling the knee close to the chest, while simultaneously using the same-side arm to gunt to further protect P1's head against the roundhouse kick. As P1 intercepts P2's kick, P1 is positioned to deliver a simulated heel kick to P2's groin.

2. Reverse the above drill using a right kick (P2 is positioned to P1's left side).

STRATEGY INSIGHT: DEFENDING AGAINST MULTIPLE STANDING ATTACKERS ADMINISTERING KICKS

This is truly one of the most dangerous positions in which to find oneself. Unless you can return to your feet immediately to flee or, out of necessity, take on multiple attackers while standing, you can easily be stomped into submission and severely injured. Many people have died as multiple attackers have literally kicked the victim to death. To prevent serious injury or death—basically putting yourself at a violent crowd's mercy—you must maneuver away from the center of the crowd. Keep moving to avoid becoming a static target. If possible, close in on an attacker and try to put him in between you and the other attackers. To counterattack this attacker, however, you must to debilitate him the best you can and get to your feet.

SEVEN

DEFENSES AGAINST HEADBUTTS

IF YOUR ATTACKER SLAMS THE HARDEST PART OF HIS HEAD—THE FOREHEAD—

INTO YOUR HEAD, THE ATTACKER CAN INFLICT SERIOUS DAMAGE. HEADBUTTS

CAN HAVE A DEBILITATING EFFECT ON A VICTIM, OFTEN TAKING THE VICTIM BY

SURPRISE. THE PRIMARY TARGETS OF THE HEADBUTT INCLUDE THE NOSE, EYE socket, and ear. The strike is optimally delivered with the front crown of the skull or the thickest frontal area of the forehead. The back of the head may also be used with devastating effect against the front of someone else's face.

BODY DEFENSE AGAINST A HEADBUTT

If you are caught in the "-5" and recognize the incoming headbutt late, you may use a body defense to move your head off the line of attack, while simultaneously striking the attacker in the groin.

The attacker was able to somehow close the distance and come within your danger zone. As you recognize the incoming headbutt, immediately move your head to the left (or right) off the line of attack. Your hands are in a natural position to strike the attacker's groin.

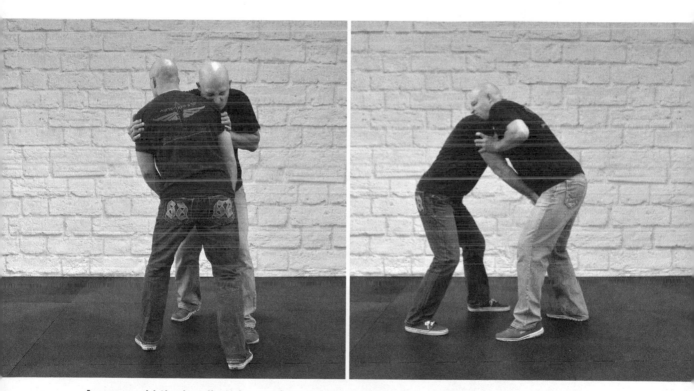

As you avoid the headbutt by moving your head off the line of attack (you may move to your left or right), cupping your hands, attack the attacker's groin. For optimum effect, slap the attacker underneath the attacker's scrotum accompanied by additional retzev combatives as necessary.

BODY DEFENSE AGAINST A HEADBUTT

This drill requires two partners, P1 (the "Defender" [you]) and P2 ("Attacker" [your partner]). P1 faces P2 about one foot apart simulating a confrontation where P2 initiates as the aggressor. Practitioners should repeat this drill a minimum of 15 repetitions for both right and left body defense evasions (30 repetitions total).

1. Against P2's headbutt attempt, P1 moves P1's head to the side, while simultaneously delivering a simulated double-hand strike to P2's groin. As you continue to improve your skill set and capabilities, finish with immediate retzev continuous combat motion counterattacks.

2. Reverse the above drill using an opposite side head movement.

UPPERCUT ELBOW DEFENSE AGAINST A HEADBUTT

A simple raised elbow parallel to the ground puts a formidable obstacle and deterrent against your attacker delivering a headbutt. It also provides you with the ability to strike.

As you recognize the incoming headbutt, raise your elbow in an uppercut fashion with your triceps parallel to the ground to block and simultaneously deliver a blow to your attacker's incoming head. Follow up with additional retzev combatives as necessary.

UPPERCUT ELBOW DEFENSE AGAINST A HEADBUTT DRILL

This drill requires two partners, P1 (the "Defender" [you]) and P2 ("Attacker" [your partner]). P1 faces P2 about one-foot apart simulating a confrontation where P2 initiates as the aggressor. Practitioners should repeat this drill a minimum of 15 repetitions for both right and uppercut elbows (30 repetitions total).

1. Against P2's headbutt attempt, P1 uses a simulated uppercut elbow defense against P2's incoming head. As you continue to improve your skill set and capabilities, finish with immediate retzev continuous combat motion counterattacks.

2. Reverse the above drill using the opposite simulated uppercut elbow strike.

HORIZONTAL ELBOW DEFENSE AGAINST A HEADBUTT

Similar to the previous defense, bringing your elbow defensively across your face puts a formidable obstacle and deterrent to your attacker delivering a headbutt. It also provides you with the ability to strike.

As you recognize the incoming headbutt, respond as if you were delivering a horizontal (#1) elbow strike.

This defensive elbow/strike shield serves the dual purpose of shielding you and simultaneously delivering a strong blow to the attacker's incoming head. Follow up with additional retzev combatives as necessary.

HORIZONTAL ELBOW DEFENSE AGAINST A HEADBUTT

This drill requires two partners, P1 (the "Defender" [you]) and P2 ("Attacker" [your partner]). P1 faces P2 about one foot apart simulating a confrontation where P2 initiates as the aggressor. P1 and P2 are facing one another. Practitioners should repeat this drill a minimum of 15 repetitions for both right and left horizontal elbows (30 repetitions total).

1. Against P2's headbutt attempt, P1 uses a simulated horizontal elbow movement defense against P2's incoming head. As you continue to improve your skill set and capabilities, finish with immediate retzev continuous combat motion counterattacks.

2. Reverse the above drill using the opposite simulated horizontal elbow movement.

FOREARM BRACE DEFENSE AGAINST A HEADBUTT

By shooting your forearm across the attacker's clavicle and the side of your neck, you can effectively create a brace to prevent the attacker's head from reaching you.

Thrust your right forearm across your attacker's throat where your elbow is bent slightly beyond 90 degrees. This movement serves the dual purpose of applying a defensive brace and counterattacking blow to your attacker's neck. Strike the attacker hard in the attacker's neck/throat with the underside of your forearm or the ulna bone. Your right shoulder is directly across from the attacker's right shoulder, with your forearm planted across the attacker's throat. Notice that this body positioning prevents the attacker from reaching you with a headbutt, but allows you to reach the attacker with your own headbutt, should you choose. Continue to counterattack with a knee to groin or any other retzev combatives of your choice.

FOREARM BRACE DEFENSE AGAINST A HEADBUTT DRILL

This drill requires two partners, P1 (the "Defender" [you]) and P2 ("Attacker" [your partner]). P1 faces P2 about one foot apart simulating a confrontation where P2 initiates as the aggressor. P1 and P2 are facing one another. Practitioners should repeat this drill a minimum of 15 repetitions using both a right brace and then a left brace (30 repetitions total).

1. Against P2's headbutt attempt, P1 shoots P1's right arm diagonally across P2's incoming head. As you continue to improve your skill set and capabilities, finish with immediate retzev continuous combat motion counterattacks.

2. Reverse the above drill using the opposite simulated diagonal brace elbow strike.

EIGHT

CHOKE AND
HEADLOCK RELEASES

A CHOKE CAN QUICKLY RENDER YOU UNCONSCIOUS OR WORSE. OF COURSE, IF

YOU RECOGNIZE SOMEONE ATTEMPTING TO CHOKE YOU, YOU COULD PREEMPT

THE ATTACKER BY USING A LOWER-BODY LONG-RANGE KICK OR AN UPPER-BODY

COUNTERATTACK OR BY DEFLECTING THE ATTACKER'S HANDS AS THE ATTACKER reaches for your throat. Yet, as long as you can still breathe, you can fight back. Krav maga's choke defenses build on instinct and are particularly illustrative of Imi Lichtenfeld's practical approach to self-defense. Most people, for example, will reach for their throats when choking on a piece of food. Similarly, if a garment is too tight around your neck, you will automatically pull down on the constricting material to give yourself breathing room.

FRONT CHOKE HOLD RELEASES

This defense, by design, is almost identical to the horizontal elbow defense against a headbutt that you learned in chapter 7 (see page 154).

The attacker was able to somehow close the distance and come within your danger zone. As you recognize the incoming choke, bury your chin into your chest while keeping your eyes up to maintain your vision. The attacker will likely drive you backward forcing you to take a natural step. When you are pushed backward to balance yourself, you will likely bring your arms up. Krav maga builds on this instinct. If you were not able to preempt the attacker from getting his hands around your throat, immediately pluck the attacker's right arm with your left hand, making sure to cup your hand.

As the attacker attempts to secure your throat, with your left hand pluck the attacker's right hand, as you pivot forward on your right leg and execute a modified horizontal elbow to release the attacker's grip. As you pluck the attacker's right hand away from your throat, simultaneously use your right arm (simulating a modified horizontal elbow strike) to come across your face to forcibly remove the attacker's left hand from your throat. Be sure to use a correct elbow clear by keeping the underside of your forearm parallel to the ground. In other words, don't shoot your right arm up into the air and try to clear the attacker's left arm with your triceps muscle (a common mistake). The modified elbow should bring your elbow up slightly with your bicep close to your ear, as you pivot strongly approximately 180 degrees. This 180-degree pivot also adds a body defense by turning your neck away from the attacker's grasp. This cuts off access to your throat and simultaneously removes the danger of an attacker's hands around your neck.

As soon as you clear the attacker's hands, use your right arm to counterattack, either using a forearm chop to the side of the attacker's neck or the other option of an elbow strike to the attacker's ear.

Continue with counterattacks such as a straight kick with your front right leg. It is optimum to use your front right leg because you took a step back with your left leg, thereby loading your weight onto it. Remember, it is always easier to kick with the leg that does not have your full weight bearing on it. Your rear base leg will probably slide a bit to accommodate your straight kick or knee to the attacker's groin. Follow up with additional retzev combatives as necessary.

FRONT CHOKE HOLD RELEASES DRILL

This drill requires two partners, P1 (the "Defender" [you]) and P2 ("Attacker" [your partner]). P1 faces P2 about one to three feet apart simulating a confrontation where P2 initiates as the aggressor. Practitioners should repeat this drill a minimum of 15 repetitions.

1. Against P2's front hand choke attempt, P1 steps back with the left leg while plucking P2's right arm with P1's left hand and clearing P2's left hand by using a modified horizontal elbow strike. P1 counterattacks by using a side elbow strike or forearm chop. P1 continues the counterattack with a right kick to P2's groin. As you continue to improve your skill set and capabilities, finish with immediate retzev continuous combat motion counterattacks.

2. Reverse the above drill by P1 stepping back with the opposite right leg and clearing with the opposite left arm.

SIDE HEADLOCK RELEASE

The side headlock can jolt your neck and place you in a vulnerable position. This attack is common and often demonstrated on the playground. Your attacker can drop his weight to the ground to exert great force on your neck while forcing you down with the attacker. Alternatively, the attacker can torque your neck causing serious harm. The attacker could also punch you in the face repeatedly with the attacker's opposite arm or drive your head into a wall. As for all defenses, the best defense against a headlock is to avoid being put into one.

Reacting at the earliest possible moment is crucial. Against a side headlock you could preempt the attack by delivering a side kick or ducking beneath the grab as the attacker moves in on you. If you see the headlock coming in, tuck your chin and turn it slightly to the right. Then wage a preemptive defense by bracing your right arm across the attacker's neck or face, attacking the eyeball.

Bring your right arm behind the attacker's back and over the attacker's left shoulder to hook the attacker's eye with your most convenient finger, while simultaneously using your left arm to deliver slaps to the groin using a cupped hand. (Other options are to use your middle and pointer fingers to reach under the attacker's nose and drive the attacker's philtrum straight back or grab the attacker's hair to leverage the head back.) Do not push against the attacker's chin, as most people can resist this pressure. If possible, prevent the attacker from clasping his hands together by timing your defense correctly, or, alternatively, using your right arm to stop the attacker's lower hand from grasping his other arm. Proceed with the groin counterattack. This will work effectively against most people; however, some people can withstand this pressure and will continue their attack.

Bring the attacker's head back by pushing deep into the attacker's eye socket, exposing the attacker's throat to a web-hand strike or any other attack from your free arm.

SIDE HEADLOCK RELEASE DRILL

This drill requires two partners, P1 (the "Defender" [you]) and P2 ("Attacker" [your partner]). P1 and P2 are facing in the same direction about one to three feet apart simulating a confrontation where P2 initiates as the aggressor. Practitioners should repeat this drill a minimum of 15 repetitions for both right and left side headlocks (30 repetitions total).

1. Against P2's side headlock attempt, P1 using the left arm reaches around P2's head, targeting the nose or eye with P1's middle fingers (not the chin) while simultaneously attacking P2's groin with his left hand. P1 may continue to counterattack by striking P2 in the face or throat (only if necessary). As you continue to improve your skill set and capabilities, finish with immediate retzev continuous combat motion counterattacks.

2. Reverse the above drill using the opposite side headlock.

DEFENSE AGAINST A SIDE HEADLOCK WHEN AN ATTACKER IS ATTEMPTING TO PUNCH THE DEFENDER

This defense (not depicted) counters an attacker putting you in a right side headlock with one arm and attempting to punch you in the face with his other arm.

Once again, reacting at the earliest possible moment is crucial. Similar to the previous defense, if you see the headlock coming in, tuck your chin and turn it slightly to the right. Then wage a preemptive defense by bracing your right arm across the attacker's neck or face, attacking the eyeball. Bring your right arm behind the attacker's back and over the attacker's left shoulder to hook his eye with your most convenient finger. (Other options are to use your middle and pointer fingers to reach under the attacker's nose and drive the attacker's philtrum straight back or grab the attacker's hair to leverage the head back.) As you attack the attacker's eye or philtrum with your right arm, shoot your left arm parallel to the ground, pointing all of your fingers in the same direction to prevent the attacker from using his arm to punch you. In other words, you are knifing your arm above the attacker's arm to prevent freedom of action for the attacker to punch you in the face with the attacker's left arm. Proceed with the groin attack and defeat the attack as necessary.

FOREARM CHOKE RELEASE FROM BEHIND

Forearm chokes (also called blood chokes) from the rear are some of the most effective and dangerous strangulation techniques. This choke can crush your windpipe or cut off the blood flow from the carotid arteries to the brain. These are powerful chokes, because the attacker's entire body can be maneuvered to exert maximum force. You must react instantaneously by tactile feel to these highly effective offensive techniques.

As soon as you sense or feel the attacker's arm, tuck your chin and turn it slightly in the direction of the attacker's interlocked hands. Turn toward the side where the attacker's hands are clasped, while immediately raising your arms to catch the attacker's forearm.

Simultaneously, with both of your hands, locate and grasp the attacker's forearm that the attacker is trying to insert under your chin. Yank down with both of your arms, with your hands as close as possible to the attacker's interlocked hands. Keep your thumb attached to your hand as you use your entire body to pull down on the attacker's forearm by dropping your weight slightly. Clear the arm forcefully from your chin/neck area.

As soon as you create slight separation, dip your left shoulder and step backward with your left leg while wheeling your right shoulder in the direction of your attacker's right shoulder. Continue to step through and underneath the attacker's right armpit while holding the attacker's arm firmly pinned against your body with both of your arms.

Immediately deliver a knee from your rear leg to the attacker's exposed head or midsection, followed by additional retzev counterattacks.

Note: If you cannot release immediately from the blood choke from the rear, revert to a modified side headlock release (page 163), but do not release your arms from the attacker's forearm until you can breathe enough to execute the side headlock release. This modified release keeps your inside (right) arm exerting as much pressure as you can on the attacker's forearm under your chin. While keeping pressure on your attacker's choking arm with your initial defense, turn into the attacker with your outside (right) leg and deliver multiple attacks to the attacker's groin with your left hand. Once you have "loosened up" your attacker, you have the option of your regular side headlock release.

Yet another variation (not depicted) of the rear and blood choke releases might involve an assailant grabbing you from behind, with one hand covering your mouth and the other arm gripping your far-side arm. To release, pluck the hand from your mouth and turn toward your assailant, toward your arm the attacker is securing. In other words, you are plucking in one direction and pivoting your body toward your assailant in the other direction (see *Advanced Krav Maga*, page 165).

FOREARM CHOKE RELEASE FROM BEHIND DRILL

This drill requires two partners, P1 (the "Defender" [you]) and P2 ("Attacker" [your partner]). P2 is proximate to P1's rear simulating a confrontation where P2 initiates as the aggressor. Practitioners should repeat this drill a minimum of 15 repetitions for both right and left arm chokes (30 repetitions total).

1. Against P2's rear right forearm choke attempt, P1 tucks P1's chin while turning P1's head to the left as P1 simultaneously yanks down with both arms on P2's right choking arm. As P1 creates separation, P1 dips down to the left, pulling P1's head through the opening between P2's arm and torso. P1 steps back and through the opening to pin P2's arm to the side. P1 counterattacks using multiple knee strikes to P2's midsection and thigh. As you continue to improve your skill set and capabilities, finish with immediate retzev continuous combat motion counterattacks.

2. Reverse the above drill using the opposite side left forearm choke.

PROFESSIONAL CHOKE RELEASE

A "professional" variation of the blood choke hold involves the attacker applying one arm underneath your chin, while snaking the other arm around the back of your head and gripping his own bicep. This is a strong hold, especially when the attacker draws back with the choking arm while pressing forward with the rear arm.

The choke release is similar to that discussed previously in the initial steps, except that *you turn into* the crook of the attacker's elbow. As you turn into the crook of the attacker's elbow, bury your chin and immediately grasp the attacker's upper forearm and lower bicep with your hands. Keep your elbows in to harness all of your core power to place counterpressure against the choke.

Continue to turn into the attacker's choking arm. As you continue to turn, wrap or "marry" your lower leg and calf to the attacker's leg. It is crucial that your keep your leg snug against the attacker's for the pending takedown and pivot on the ball of your foot. Importantly, if you do not keep your leg braced against the attacker, he can turn with you to continue applying the choke, and the technique will not work. As you continue with your counterpressure using your arms and approximate 180-degree body turn/leg wrap, now step forward with your left leg and step down onto the heel of your right leg to drive the attacker to the attacker's right corner. (The right corner concept here is a takedown principle often associated with judo.) If the attacker is exceptionally large or strong, you may need to shift your weight to your left leg, pulling the attacker with you, thereby forcing the attacker to load the attacker's weight on his right leg. This weight-shifting tactic will facilitate your wrapping your leg around the attacker's to take the attacker down and break the choke.

Unbalance the attacker by driving the attacker to the attacker's left corner with strong counterpressure. (Do not simply force the attacker backward.) Take the attacker down hard.

Administer a heel kick and additional retzev combatives
as necessary to defeat the threat.

PROFESSIONAL CHOKE RELEASE FROM BEHIND DRILL

This drill requires two partners, P1 (the "Defender" [you]) and P2 ("Attacker" [your partner]). P2
is proximate to P1's rear simulating a confrontation where P2 initiates as the aggressor. Practitio
ners should repeat this drill a minimum of 15 repetitions for both right and left arm chokes (30
repetitions total).

1. Against P2's rear right forearm professional choke attempt, P1 tucks P1's chin while turning the
   head to the right, as P1 simultaneously yanks down with both arms on the crook of P2's right
   choking arm, keeping P1's arms tight to P1's torso. As P1 creates separation, P1 simultaneously
   wraps or marries P1's right leg to P2's right leg. P1 steps forward with the left leg and continues
   to turn, trapping P2's leg to take P2 down to break the choke hold. P1 counterattacks using a
   minimum of one heel stomp.

2. Reverse the above drill using the opposite side left professional arm choke.

PROFESSIONAL CHOKE ALTERNATIVE RELEASE

In the event you turn into the attacker's clasped hands, you can use a similar defense to the forearm choke release covered previously (see pages 166–68).

On feeling an attacker attempt to wrap his arm around your neck, immediately tuck your chin and bring your arms up to thwart the choke attempt.

Take your right hand and place it as close as you can to the attacker's folded arm (to the left of your chin) to apply core counterpressure. Be sure not to secure the attacker's arm close to the crook of the attacker's right elbow, as this does not facilitate optimum counterpressure. Your left hand simultaneously locates the attacker's hand clasping the attacker's own bicep to immediately yank down on the attacker's fingers to release the attacker's grip, thereby relieving some of the choking pressure.

As soon as you feel you have alleviated the choking pressure, let go of the attacker's fingers and deliver a sharp, powerful #6 rear low elbow or series of elbows to the attacker's groin. As the elbow strike takes effect, dip your left shoulder and step backward with your left leg while wheeling your right shoulder in the direction of your attacker's right shoulder.

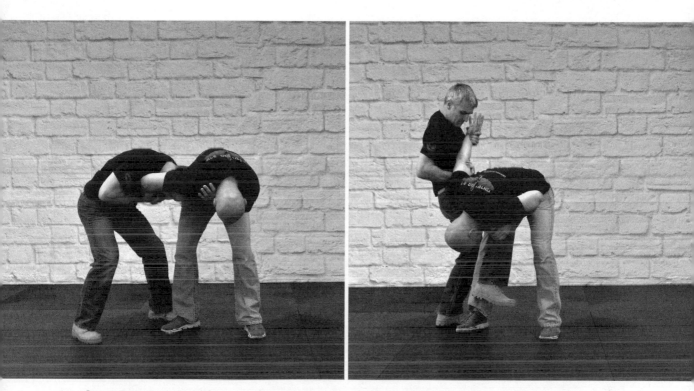

As you create separation, continue to step through and underneath the attacker's right armpit while holding the attacker's arm firmly pinned against your body with both of your arms. Immediately deliver a knee from your rear leg to the attacker's exposed midsection followed by additional retzev counterattacks.

PROFESSIONAL CHOKE ALTERNATIVE RELEASE
FROM BEHIND DRILL

This drill requires two partners, P1 (the "Defender" [you]) and P2 ("Attacker" [your partner]). P2 is to P1's rear simulating a confrontation where P2 initiates as the aggressor. Practitioners should repeat this drill a minimum of 15 repetitions for both right and left arm chokes (30 repetitions total).

1. Against P2's rear right forearm professional choke attempt, P1 tucks P1's chin while yanking down on P2's right arm with P1's right arm close to P2's folded arm. P1 also simultaneously yanks down on P2's left bicep and hand to help create separation. As P1 feels a slight separation, P1 releases the right counterpressure hand and attacks P2 in the groin using hand or elbow strikes. As P1 creates separation, P1 dips down to the left pulling P1's head through the opening between P2's arm and torso. P1 steps back and through the opening to pin P2's arm to the side. P1 counterattacks using multiple knee strikes to P2's midsection and thigh. As you continue to improve your skill set and capabilities, finish with immediate retzev continuous combat motion counterattacks.

2. Reverse the above drill using the opposite side left professional arm choke.

NINE

DEFENDING TACKLE-TYPE TAKEDOWNS

ONE OF THE MOST TYPICAL ASSAULTS IS A TACKLE TYPE OF TAKEDOWN USED BY

TRAINED AND UNTRAINED FIGHTERS, ESPECIALLY GROUND FIGHTERS. THIS TAKE-

DOWN IS DESIGNED TO PUT AN OPPONENT DOWN HARD ON HIS BACK AND HEAD

WITH THE TACKLER IN A STRONG POSITION TO CONTINUE AN ATTACK. A TACKLE takedown can smash you into a wall or put you on the ground quickly, with your attacker on top of you ready to pummel you. If taken down, your foremost concern must be to protect your head by tucking your chin and doing your best to execute the rear fall break. (A "fall break" is a fall that is performed in a tactical manner so as to both avoid personal injury as well as open yourself to injury from the attacker.) You can defend against a takedown tackle using several methods, depending on when you recognize the impending takedown threat.

STRAIGHT OFFENSIVE KICK TO THE FACE

If you recognize a tackle takedown attack early enough, launch a rear straight kick to the attacker's face. Note that accomplished ground fighters train to overcome this technique by deflecting the kick and continuing with the takedown.

As soon as you recognize the impending attack, begin to calibrate the distance and time the attacker will take to reach you. With correct timing, pivot 180 degrees on the ball of your front foot to deliver a powerful rear kick, while keeping your hands up. Deliver the kick directly through the attacker's face, curling your toes and using the ball of your foot.

As you jolt the attacker backward with your straight kick, land forward on the ball of your right foot touching down, keeping your weight distributed on your now rear left leg. Harness your momentum to deliver a subsequent straight knee strike with your patella to the attacker's head. Follow up with additional retzev combatives as necessary. As an alternative, you may simply use a left leg kick against a target of opportunity.

This drill requires two partners, P1 (the "Defender" [you]) and P2 ("Attacker" [your partner]). P1 faces P2 about three to six feet apart simulating a confrontation where P2 initiates as the aggressor. Practitioners should repeat this drill a minimum of 15 repetitions per kicking leg.

1. Against P2's tackle takedown attempt, P1 delivers a simulated straight rear timing kick to P2's face without making contact.

2. This variation requires a suitable kicking pad or shield. Against P2's simulated tackle takedown attempt that can be signaled by P2 using a stomp (enabling P2 to hold the pad firmly), P1 delivers rear straight timing kicks using 25%, 50%, and 100% power and explosion. The pad holder, P2, should exhale on contact similar to step #1.

3. A variation of this drill may be using a hanging heavy bag where P2 stands behind the bag and pushes the bag forward to simulate an attacker initiating a tackle takedown. P1 delivers various levels of power as noted above.

4. As you improve your skill set and capabilities, you may then bolster your defense by adding:

    a. Two straight kicks or a kick and then knee combination.

    b. Two straight kicks and stomp (as P2 simulates) dropping as a result of the knee.

    c. A straight kick and same-side straight punch or palm heel combination. In other words, if you kick with your right leg as soon as your foot makes contact with the target, initiate a straight punch or palm heel strike followed by additional punches, elbow strikes, knees, kicks, etc.

    d. Rear kick and turn into straight kick variation to finish with retzev continuous combat motion counterattacks.

Note: A variation of this drill can be used to defend against your partner attacking with straight punches, grabs, and chokes.

STRAIGHT OFFENSIVE KNEE TO THE FACE

If you recognize a tackle takedown within knee range, launch a rear straight knee to the attacker's face. Accomplished ground fighters train to overcome this technique by deflecting the knee and continuing with the tackle or takedown. Note: The knee is used when the distance is shorter and the attacker has closed on you too quickly for the straight kick option.

Similar to previous rear straight kick defense, as soon as your recognize the impending attack, begin to calibrate the distance and time the attacker will take to reach you. With correct timing, pivot 180 degrees on the ball of your front foot to deliver a powerful rear knee strike while keeping your hands up. Deliver the knee directly through the attacker's face, curling your toes and using the ball of your foot. Follow up with additional retzev combatives as necessary.

SIDESTEP BODY DEFENSE WITH A DOUBLE-PALM HEEL JAM

If you do not have time to launch a straight offensive kick or knee to the face of an attacker set on taking you down, a body defense coupled with palm heel jam can be highly effective to control the attacker's head, which will break the angle of attack. You must execute a strong palm heel jam beginning with your near-side arm to the attacker's temple, ear, or jaw. Keep in mind that a skilled attacker will not telegraph his/her intent to take you to the ground. Rather, the attacker will disguise his/her plan by using combatives or feints against you when you appear vulnerable. Accordingly, you must always be on the balls of your feet to (re)act.

Use a sidestep body defense to the left by pivoting your right leg 180 degrees using a tai sabaki step. Keep your hands up and prepare to jam the attacker in the side of the attacker's head, targeting the temple, ear, or jaw.

Cupping your left hand over your right hand, extend both arms, touching your hands together and cupping your hands inward to give you a strong brace against the attacker's incoming head. Jam the heels of your hands into the attacker's head as you step sideways to break the angle of attack. Follow up with an additional right rear knee strike to the head. Note: Even if the attacker has long arms and is able to wrap his arm around you, your outstretched arms using a "V" frame with a strong base stance can still control the attacker's head by inserting your pointer or middle finger into the attacker's near-side eye socket. Follow up with additional retzev combatives as necessary.

This drill requires two partners, P1 (the "Defender" [you]) and P2 ("Attacker" [your partner]). P1 faces P2 about three to six feet apart simulating a confrontation where P2 initiates as the aggressor. Practitioners should repeat this drill a minimum of 15 repetitions per pivot side (15 times with a left pivot and 15 times with right pivot [30 repetitions total]). For each drill, finish with retzev continuous combat motion counterattacks.

1. Against P2's tackle takedown attempt, P1 uses correct timing and footwork to defend the takedown by using a tai sabaki sidestep while using both palm heels (left cupped on top of the right) to deliver a simulated palm heel jam to P2's ear, jaw, or temple making only light contact.

2. This variation drill uses a small strike pad where, in a crouch, P2 moves toward P1 and presents the pad for P1 to deliver a palm heel strike in combination with proper footwork.

3. This variation drill uses a heavy hanging bag that P1 may use while training alone to combine proper footwork while delivering a palm heel strike using 25%, 50%, and 100% power and explosion.

4. This variation drill uses a heavy hanging bag with P2 standing behind the bag. P2 can signal a simulated tackle takedown attempt by moving the bag toward P1. P1 may use the bag while training alone to combine proper footwork, while delivering a palm heel strike using 25%, 50%, and 100% power and explosion.

SIDESTEP BOXING DEFENSE AGAINST A DOUBLE LEG TAKEDOWN

Similar to the previous palm heel jam defense, this defense uses footwork and straight punches (or palm heel strikes) to the temple, jaw, and neck to defeat an attempt to take you to the ground.   If you do not have time to launch a straight offensive kick or knee to the face of an attacker set on taking you down, a body defense coupled with a one-two punch combination to the attacker's head targeting the temple, ear, or jaw followed immediately by a knee to the head is highly effective. You must execute the one-two punch combination beginning with your near-side front arm to the attacker's temple, ear or jaw. Once again, keep in mind that a skilled attacker will not telegraph his/her intent to take you to the ground. Rather, the attacker will disguise his/her plan by using combatives or feints against you when you appear vulnerable. So, always be on the balls of your feet to (re)act.

Use a sideways body defense to the left by pivoting your right leg 180 degrees using a tai sabaki step. Keep your hands up and prepare to punch the attacker in the side of the attacker's head, targeting the temple, ear, or jaw.

Deliver a lead left punch to the attacker's temple, ear, or jaw, transferring your weight correctly through the punch.

After your left punch, instantaneously follow up with a rear punch, making sure to once again transfer your weight correctly through the punch. Be sure to account for the attacker's continued forward movement and momentum or "time in motion." Follow up with an additional right rear knee strike to the head. Note: Even if the attacker has long arms and is able wrap his arm around you, your outstretched arms with a strong base can still control the attacker's head by inserting your pointer or middle finger into the attacker's near-side eye socket. Follow up with additional retzev combatives as necessary. Note: If the attacker is able to secure your front leg, transfer your weight to that leg and embed your fingers into the attacker's closest eye to create separation. As always, follow up with retzev combatives as necessary.

This drill requires two partners, P1 (the "Defender" [you]) and P2 ("Attacker" [your partner]). P1 faces P2 about three to six feet apart simulating a confrontation where P2 initiates as the aggressor. Practitioners should repeat this drill a minimum of 15 repetitions per pivot side (15 times with a left pivot and 15 times with a right pivot [30 repetitions total]). For each drill, finish with retzev continuous combat motion counterattacks.

1. Against P2's tackle takedown attempt, P1 uses correct timing and footwork to defend the takedown by using a tai sabaki sidestep while delivering correct form straight punches to P2's ear, jaw, or temple, making no contact.

2. Against P2's tackle takedown attempt, P1 uses correct timing and footwork to defend the takedown by using a tai sabaki sidestep while delivering correct form palm heel strikes to P2's ear, jaw, or temple making light contact.

3. This variation drill uses a small strike pad where, in a crouch, P2 moves toward P1 and presents the pad for P1 to deliver a one-two left-right straight punch combination with proper footwork followed by a right straight knee to the pad (simulating the head).

4. This variation drill uses a heavy hanging bag that P1 may use while training alone to combine proper footwork while delivering a one-two left-right straight punch combination with proper footwork followed by a right straight knee to the bag using 25%, 50%, and 100% power and explosion.

5. This variation drill uses a heavy hanging bag with P2 standing behind the bag. P2 can signal a simulated tackle takedown attempt by moving the bag toward P1. P1 may use the bag while training alone to combine proper footwork, while delivering a one-two left-right straight punch combination with proper footwork followed by a right straight knee using 25%, 50%, and 100% power and explosion.

FOREARM WEDGE JAM TO THE ATTACKER'S NECK

With correct timing and positioning, you can also use an instinctive forearm jam against the attacker's throat. Note: This defense may be used when you recognize the attack late and must react instinctively as it does not involve much of a body defense.

From a fighting stance, use the underside of your forearm (the ulna) to jam and strike the attacker's neck at the brachial plexus as the attacker sinks his level to take you down. It is crucial that you keep your arm bent beyond 90 degrees to make use of your extensor muscles to create a strong brace to keep the attacker away from your torso. As you deliver the forearm jam and strike with your legs, you should shoot slightly backward in a continued strong fighting stance to withstand the attacker's forward leg drive against your torso. Follow up with additional retzev combatives as necessary.

FOREARM WEDGE JAM TO THE ATTACKER'S NECK DRILL

This drill requires two partners, P1 (the "Defender" [you]) and P2 ("Attacker" [your partner]). P1 faces P2 about three to six feet apart simulating a confrontation where P2 initiates as the aggressor. Practitioners should repeat this drill a minimum of 15 repetitions per pivot side (15 times with a left pivot and 15 times with a right pivot [30 repetitions total]). For each drill, finish with retzev continuous combat motion counterattacks.

1. Against P2's tackle takedown attempt, P1 uses correct timing and footwork to defend the takedown using a simulated forearm jam to P2's ear, jaw, or temple making no contact.

2. Against P2's tackle takedown attempt, P1 uses correct timing and footwork to defend the takedown using a simulated forearm jam to P2's ear, jaw, or temple making light contact.

3. This variation drill uses a small strike pad where, in a crouch, P2 moves toward P1 and presents the pad for P1 to deliver using a simulated forearm jam.

4. This variation drill uses a heavy hanging bag that P1 may use while training alone to combine proper footwork while delivering a simulated forearm jam using 25%, 50%, and 100% power and explosion.

5. This variation drill uses a heavy hanging bag with P2 standing behind the bag. P2 can signal a simulated tackle takedown attempt by moving the bag toward P1. P1 practices by using a simulated forearm jam followed by a right straight knee using 25%, 50%, and 100% power and explosion.

OUTSIDE SPRAWL #1 BY SHOOTING THE HIPS BACK WITH COMBATIVES

Outside (and inside) sprawls are used when you cannot react with a leg counterattack or by sidestepping, either because your reaction is late or, perhaps, the attacker feinted some kind of other attack and then moved in to take you down. Sprawling backward keeping your weight on the balls of your feet allows you to create superior leverage, preventing the attacker from reaching your legs.

As you recognize the incoming takedown, if you have not already done so, transfer your weight to the balls of your feet. As the attacker closes the distance, begin to lower your right arm to provide the "brakes" to stop the attacker from reaching your legs. For this variation your torso is directly in line with the attacker's torso.

As the attacker lunges and you intercept with your right arm, shoot your hips back dropping one arm to the ground to apply the "brakes" and lean your upper torso forward, placing all of your body weight on the attacker's head and upper torso. By dropping one arm you prevent the attacker from continuing underneath your torso to grab your legs. Be sure to spread your legs wide and remain on the balls of your feet.

The attacker will fall facedown, putting you in an advantageous position for counterattacks including eye rakes, neck manipulations, elbow strikes, chokes, or a knee to the back top of the head. Follow up with additional retzev combatives as necessary.

OUTSIDE SPRAWL #1 BY SHOOTING THE HIPS BACK WITH COMBATIVES DRILL

This drill requires two partners, P1 (the "Defender" [you]) and P2 ("Attacker" [your partner]). P1 faces P2 about three to six feet apart simulating a confrontation where P2 initiates as the aggressor. Practitioners should repeat this drill a minimum of 15 repetitions per "brakes arm" side (15 times with a left arm drop and 15 times with a right arm drop [30 repetitions total]). For each drill, finish with retzev continuous combat motion counterattacks.

1. Against P2's tackle takedown attempt, P1 uses correct timing and footwork to defend the takedown using a simulated "outside" sprawl landing P1's weight on P2's upper back with P1's legs correctly sprawled back and away. P1 simulates face rips and straight knees to P2's head without making contact to P2's head and then P1 rises to P1's feet immediately.

2. An exercise version of this drill may be performed alone whereby P1 sprawls into a push-up position (keeping the elbows in) with the legs properly sprawled back and then gets up immediately. P1 may perform this drill 15 times (or more) in a row with short rest periods in between. A minimum of 3 sets is recommended.

INSIDE SPRAWL #2 BY SHOOTING THE HIPS BACK WITH COMBATIVES

Once again, if you cannot react with a leg counterattack or by sidestepping, you can apply the brakes and shoot your hips back, dropping one arm to the ground to intercept the tackle while leaning your upper torso forward, placing all or your body weight on the attacker's head and upper torso. This variation allows you get up immediately and use a power heel kick to debilitate the attacker.

As you recognize the incoming takedown, if you have not already, transfer your weight to the balls of your feet. As the attacker closes the distance, begin to lower your right arm to provide the brakes to stop the attacker from reaching your legs. For this variation, your torso is not directly in line with the attacker's torso, but rather slightly off to one side. Once again, sprawling backward, while keeping your weight on the balls of your feet, with your legs spread wide, allows you to create superior leverage, preventing the attacker from reaching your legs. By dropping your near-side arm, you prevent the attacker from continuing underneath your torso to grab your legs.

The attacker will fall facedown, putting you in an advantageous position to get up immediately and kick the attacker in the head with your heel or ball of the foot.

If an attacker is successful in closing on you and grapples with you, immediately transition to anatomical targeting. In other words, attack whatever vulnerable anatomy is accessible. For example, if the attacker forces you to rear attack his eyes using the rule of thumb or if your arms are pinned, attack the attacker's groin. If you fall with your attacker, place your knee in the attacker's groin as you both descend. More of these tactics are covered in the next chapter focusing on bear hug releases.

INSIDE SPRAWL #2 BY SHOOTING THE HIPS BACK WITH COMBATIVES DRILL

This drill requires two partners, P1 (the "Defender" [you]) and P2 ("Attacker" [your partner]). P1 faces P2 about three to six feet apart simulating a confrontation where P2 initiates as the aggressor. Practitioners should repeat this drill a minimum of 15 repetitions per "brakes arm side" side (15 times with a left arm drop and 15 times with a right arm drop [30 repetitions total]). For each drill, finish with retzev continuous combat motion counterattacks.

1. Against P2's tackle takedown attempt, P1 uses correct timing and footwork to defend the takedown using a simulated "inside" sprawl landing P1's weight on P2's upper back with P1's legs correctly sprawled back and away. P1 simulates getting up immediately to simulate a stomp to P2's head without making contact.

2. An exercise version of this drill may be performed alone whereby P1 sprawls into a push-up position (keeping the elbows in) with the legs properly sprawled back and then gets up immediately. P1 may perform this drill 15 times (or more) in a row with short rest periods in between. A minimum of 3 sets is recommended.

TEN

BEAR HUG DEFENSES

FRONT BEAR HUG DEFENSES WITH THE ARMS FREE

An attacker applying a face-to-face torso grab or a bear hug can crush your ribs or pick your entire body up and smash it to the ground. The attacker may grab underneath your arms, allowing them to go free, or may pin them to your sides. The best defense against this and other high-grabbing or throwing attacks is to preempt them with a long-range kick or a knee to the attacker's groin or midsection or a medium-range straight punch. If you do get caught in a front bear hug with your arms free, the following is a readily available defense.

As you recognize the impending attack, raise both of your arms, preparing to insert your thumbs into your attacker's eye sockets. As you insert your thumbs, wrap your left (or right leg) around the attacker's same-side leg. Another option (not depicted) is to simply shoot your hips back, creating distance, and kick the attacker in the groin. Using strong pressure against the attacker's eyeballs, with your hooked leg force the attacker to his right corner. Drive the attacker in the direction of your pointed toes. As the attacker goes down, deliver a right stomp kick using your heel to the attacker's head. Continue to neutralize the threat with stomps, kicks, and additional retzev combatives.

This drill requires two partners, P1 (the "Defender" [you]) and P2 ("Attacker" [your partner]). P1 faces P2 about one foot apart simulating a confrontation where P2 initiates as the aggressor. Practitioners should repeat this drill a minimum of 15 repetitions and continue to finish with retzev continuous combat motion counterattacks as necessary.

- Against P2's front bear hug with the arms free attempt, P1 uses correct timing to simulate attacking P2's eyes while P1 simultaneously wraps a leg around P2's leg. P1 forces P2 to the corner and continues the counterattack with a stomp. P1 must be careful not to injure P2's eyes. It is suggested to place the thumbs on P2's eyebrows and have P2 close P2's eyes for safety.

FRONT BEAR HUG DEFENSES WHILE BEING LIFTED

Your chances of being lifted will be greatly reduced if you insert one of your legs inside one of the attacker's legs. Should the attacker succeed in lifting you with a bear hug (not depicted), your defenses will remain the same with a few modifications. Hook one of your outside legs tightly around your attacker's outside leg. If you are lifted from the front and your arms are free, you may do the same as the first bear hug defense. Finish with retzev counterattacks. A double-handed slap to the attacker's ears is also effective ("boxing the ears"). If you are lifted from the front and your arms are pinned, hook one leg and use the other leg to deliver knee strikes. You may also be in a position to use hand strikes to the groin, or, if necessary, bite the attacker's neck. Finish with retzev counterattacks.

FRONT BEAR HUG DEFENSES WITH THE ARMS PINNED

Once again, a face-to-face torso grab or a bear hug can crush your ribs or pick your entire body up and smash it to the ground. Your attacker may grab your arms, pinning them to your torso. Of course, the best defense against this and other high-grabbing or throwing attacks is to preempt them with a long-range kick or a knee to the attacker's groin or midsection or a medium-range straight punch. If you do get caught in a front bear hug with your arms pinned, the following is the primary defensive option.

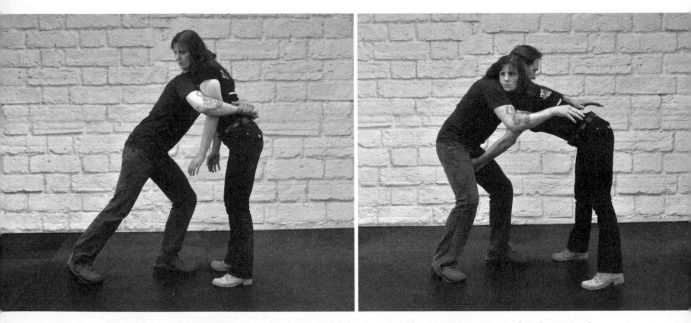

Shoot your hips back about six inches, giving yourself enough room to simultaneously insert your hands in front of your body to strike the attacker's groin. At the same time, be sure to bring your head to one side and tuck your chin into your neck to protect against an inadvertent headbutt. (A slap to your attacker's groin will likely bring the attacker's head forward.)

After multiple groin strikes, reach with both hands behind the attacker, and, using a hand pinch (grabbing and making a tight fist), grab clothing, flesh, or both and continue with knee strikes. You can also bite the attacker's neck and continue with additional strikes.

FRONT BEAR HUG DEFENSES WITH THE ARMS PINNED DRILL

This drill requires two partners, P1 (the "Defender" [you]) and P2 ("Attacker" [your partner]). P1 faces P2 about one foot apart simulating a confrontation where P2 initiates as the aggressor. Practitioners should repeat this drill a minimum of 15 repetitions and finish with retzev continuous combat motion counterattacks as necessary.

- Against P2's front bear hug pinning-the-arms attempt, P1 uses correct timing to simulate smashing P2's groin. After creating separation, P1 simulates a straight knee to P2's groin followed by additional counterattacks as necessary.

DEFENSE AGAINST FRONT BEAR HUG WITH THE ARMS FREE AND BEING DRIVEN BACK

A low front bear hug can be difficult to distinguish from a tackle. As noted, a tackle usually involves a running start, enabling the tackler to drive his body through your body and taking you backward to the ground. The low bear hug lifts and throws or squeezes the torso strongly. Yet again, the best defense against this and other high-grabbing or throwing attacks is to preempt them with a long-range kick or knee to the attacker's groin or midsection or medium-range straight punch. This highly effective defensive option, involves torquing the attacker's neck using a 180-degree tai sabaki body step and turn, placing enormous pressure on the attacker's neck. The half-circle step turns your hips and body weight against the attacker's neck. This is otherwise known as a neck crank.

As the attacker catches you and drives you back, you will naturally take a step back to balance yourself while raising your arms. Krav maga builds on this reaction. This movement creates a stronger body position to resist the push while positioning you to attacking the attacker's head. As the attacker buries his head into your torso, immediately use a modified right palm heel strike to the attacker's left cheekbone, while preparing to insert your thumb into the attacker's eye socket. Simultaneously, reach around the attacker's face to embed a finger in the attacker's eye or hook under the attacker's nose and secure your other hand against the attacker's chin. Squeeze the attacker's head into your torso.

After you firmly secure and squeeze the attacker's head to your torso while embedding your right thumb in the attacker's eye socket, take a 180-degree step back with your left front leg. This torso turn places tremendous rotational torquing stress on the attacker's neck by taking your front leg back to the rear using a tai sabaki movement. Push with your near-side right hand and pull with your far-side left hand.

Be sure not to take the attacker down and then stand over the attacker with the attacker's legs between yours, exposing your groin to kicks. A good follow-up after stepping over your downed attacker is a kick to the attacker's head with your heel. Follow up with additional retzev combatives as necessary.

FRONT BEAR HUG DEFENSES WITH NECK TORQUE DRILL

This drill requires two partners, P1 (the "Defender" [you]) and P2 ("Attacker" [your partner]). P1 faces P2 about one foot apart simulating a confrontation where P2 initiates as the aggressor. Practitioners should repeat this drill a minimum of 15 repetitions on each side of the torso (30 repetitions total) and finish with retzev continuous combat motion counterattacks as necessary.

- Against P2's front bear hug attempt (P1's arms are free), P1 uses correct timing to step back and secure P2's head. Note: For safety, this drill must be performed slowly and with extreme caution. P1 uses a correct tai sabaki step to gently rotate P2 down to the ground and follows up with a simulated stomp. Again, this drill must not be performed forcefully to protect P2's neck.

REAR BEAR HUG DEFENSE WITH YOUR ARMS FREE

A close-grab bear hug from the rear places you in great danger of being driven forward into a wall or the ground or being thrown. Note that you are especially vulnerable if you are holding a phone or have it pressed to your ear. The attacker is likely to force you forward or backward, which will naturally cause you to take a step in an attempt to maintain your balance. Whether the attacker drives you forward or pulls you in reverse, use this step to your advantage by inserting it between the attacker's legs.

As you feel the attacker slip his arms under your arms to wrap his arms around your torso pulling you backward, drop your weight, and, if possible, shoot your left leg backward between the attacker's legs from the inside to prevent the attacker from lifting you.

A split moment after you drop your weight, begin your counterattack with the same-side left elbow pivoting your body to your left. Continue with left elbow attacks by pivoting your body to your left. Immediately deliver a left straight knee to the attacker's groin once you have turned your body 180 degrees as facilitated by your multiple left rear elbow strikes. Note: You can also counterstrike with an upward "mule" kick by striking your heel into the attacker's groin. Another option is to lift one leg and smash your attacker's shin with the side of the upraised foot and then rake your foot down the attacker's shin and then stomp down on the attacker's foot. To ensure the attacker releases his hands, strike the back of the attacker's top clasped hand repeatedly as you would rap on a door. Turn and face your attacker to continue retzev counterattacks.

This drill requires two partners, P1 (the "Defender" [you]) and P2 ("Attacker" [your partner]). P2 is about one feet behind P1 simulating a confrontation where P2 initiates as the aggressor. Practitioners should repeat this drill a minimum of 15 repetitions on each side of the torso, stepping back with the left leg and then stepping back with the right leg to perform a mirror drill (30 repetitions total). Finish with retzev continuous combat motion counterattacks as necessary.

- Against P2's rear bear hug attempt (P1's arms are free), P1 uses correct timing to step back and deliver a rear horizontal elbow strike while P1 continues to turn and face the attacker. P1 should simulate a follow-up knee counterattack to P2's groin with front leg. Note: For safety, this drill must be performed slowly and with extreme caution.

REAR BEAR HUG DEFENSE WITH YOUR ARMS PINNED

A close-grab bear hug from the rear places you in grave danger of being driven forward into a wall or the ground or being thrown, especially if your arms are pinned. You are especially, vulnerable if you are texting. Once again, if the attacker pulls you backward, take a step with the attacker.

If you are texting, an attacker can easily pin your arms to your side. If the attacker is attempting to secure your arms against your torso, react immediately by bending your elbows and shooting your arms straight up to prevent the attacker from clasping his hands together around your torso. Try to keep your elbows flush to your torso and not splay them out. The attacker is likely to force you forward or backward, which will cause you to naturally take a step in an attempt to maintain your balance. Whether the attacker drives you forward or pulls you in reverse, use this step to your advantage by inserting it between the attacker's legs. As you shoot your arms up, drop your weight, and, when possible, insert of one of your legs between the attacker's legs, hooking your attacker's same-side leg from the inside.

Having prevented the attacker from wrapping his arms around you, immediately step to your left while delivering a chop or palm heel strike to the attacker's groin with your right hand and securing the attacker's left hand by his thumb. Look over your right shoulder to deliver a right rear horizontal elbow (the opposite of a forward horizontal elbow) to the attacker's head.

As you further stun the attacker with a rear horizontal #3 elbow, transition your right hand to further clasp the attacker's left hand while performing a 180-degree tai sabaki step to secure a fingerlock on the attacker.

As you partially immobilize the attacker with your fingerlock, deliver a debilitating side kick to the attacker's near-side knee. Finish with retzev counterattacks.

Note: If the attacker succeeds in securing your arms to your torso, drop your body weight instantaneously and then shift your body weight to one side or the other.

This will expose the attacker's groin. Look behind you and strike at the attacker's groin. Rapidly shift your weight to the other side, if you cannot hit the groin on the first attempt. Shifting your body weight, utilizing the strength of your lower body, and taking short emphatic steps will loosen the attacker's hold to allow your counterattack.

REAR BEAR HUG DEFENSE WITH YOUR ARMS PINNED DRILL

This drill requires two partners, P1 (the "Defender" [you]) and P2 ("Attacker" [your partner]). P2 is about one foot behind P1 simulating a confrontation where P2 initiates as the aggressor. Practitioners should repeat this drill a minimum of 15 repetitions on each side of the torso, stepping back with the left leg and then stepping back with the right leg to perform a mirror drill (30 repetitions total). Finish with retzev continuous combat motion counterattacks as necessary.

1. Against P2's rear bear hug attempt (P1's arms are free), P1 uses correct timing to step back and deliver a rear horizontal elbow strike while P1 continues to turn and face the attacker. P1 should simulate a follow-up knee counterattack to P2's groin with front leg. Note: For safety, this drill must be performed slowly and with extreme caution.

REAR BEAR HUG DEFENSE WHILE BEING LIFTED

An attacker may succeed in lifting you (not depicted) despite your best attempt to drop your weight. If your arms are free, hook your outside leg tightly to your attacker's outside leg and proceed as you would with either the arms free or arms pinned rear bear hug defenses. Consider a mule kick to the groin as well (see *Krav Maga,* page 135). Finish with retzev counterattacks. If your arms are pinned, hook your outside leg tightly around your attacker's leg and use the low front bear hug with the arms free or arms pinned defense. Finish with retzev counterattacks.

ELEVEN

TAKEN DOWN ON YOUR BACK

TAKEDOWNS AND TACKLES ARE COMMON STREET ATTACKS, ESPECIALLY IF TWO

ATTACKERS GRAPPLE WITH ONE ANOTHER, HENCE THE IMPORTANCE OF DEVELOP-

ING YOUR ANTI-TAKEDOWN CAPABILITIES TO REMAIN STANDING. IF YOU

ARE TAKEN DOWN, YOU RISK A SECOND ASSAILANT OR MULTIPLE ASSAILANTS attacking you. To state the obvious, fighting multiple adversaries on the ground is extremely difficult. In short, do not go to the ground if it can be helped.

Krav maga ground survival techniques incorporate both defensive and offensive tactics and can generally be summarized as: "What we do up, we do down." In other words, in krav maga whatever is done from an upright position is done (with modification) from a ground position. As there are no rules in an "up" fight, there are no rules in a "down" fight. Groin strikes, throat strikes, eye gouges, and biting are all viable ground-survival options.

You must be able to defend against an attacker changing his level of attack. Allowing an attacker to successfully change his level provides the attacker with the opportunity to attack your legs with significant force and speed. Successful takedowns are often set up by an attacker using a distraction (usually an upper-body strike feint). While the combative distraction may or may not connect, it will allow the attacker to lower his level with proper posture to protect his head from counterattack. Thus, a strong attack against your legs is made possible by the attacker gliding forcefully under your lead arm, while he uses his lead shoulder to make takedown contact against your hip and thighs.

In this chapter, you will learn the most important technique of all—how to fall to the ground safely. At some point during a confrontation, you may get your legs knocked out from under you, lose your balance, or trip while running. No matter what causes the fall, you need to know how to go from upright to prone without hurting yourself. Just as important, the techniques you will soon learn will help you break any type of fall, whether you slip on ice or trip over a rock while hiking.

SIDE FALL BREAK INTO THE FORELEG BRACE POSITION

If the defenses you learned in chapters 9 and 10 are not available or somehow failed to prevent the attacker from taking you down, you must fall both tactically and strategically to avoid injury and to not allow the attacker further opportunities to injure you. The side fall break prepares you to fall on your side.

As you recognize you will be taken down, prepare your body to fall on your side.

For the side fall break, you must slap the ground with the arm closest to the ground, using the same slapping motion as the rear fall break (see *Krav Maga,* pages 104–105). As you fall, tuck your chin and elevate the same-side leg (closest to the ground) to avoid your knee crashing the ground. Immediately attack the attacker using an eye gouge or other combative to the attacker's head.

By turning on your side, insert your top foreleg and knee between you and the attacker to keep the attacker at bay as you deliver combatives such as eye gouges and throat strikes. The leg "brakes" technique disengages you from an attacker who is trying to spread your legs or mount you. Remember, your hips and legs are your most powerful muscles; use them well. Prepare to deliver a heel kick to the attacker's head or solar plexus.

As you separate yourself from your attacker, you will likely gain the opportunity to kick the attacker in the head or chest using a straight heel kick or a side kick also striking with the heel. Get up as quickly as you can by sliding your left leg back and onto the ball of your foot, while posting one hand on the ground to deliver more combatives and make your escape. While engaged in the brace, you may also use your left leg to kick the attacker's groin with your heel or kick the attacker's thigh to knock the attacker's left leg out from under the attacker and then kick the attacker in the head.

The foreleg brace position allows you to defend against upper-body attacks using the same simultaneous defense and attacker principles you learned in your standing defenses, except with a few modifications.

SIDE FALL BREAK INTO THE FORELEG BRACE POSITION DRILL

This drill requires two partners, P1 (the "Defender" [you]) and P2 ("Attacker" [your partner]). P2 is about one foot in front of P1 simulating a confrontation where P2 initiates as the aggressor performing a simulated front takedown. Practitioners should repeat this drill a minimum of 15 repetitions on each side of the torso to fall back on each side for a mirror drill (30 repetitions total). Finish with retzev continuous ground survival counterattacks as necessary.

This drill should be performed on a mat or padded surface. Against P2's front takedown (P1's arms are free), P1 performs a correct fall break landing on P1's side. P1 should simulate creating separation and follow up with simulated heel kicks and other attacks to P2's head, solar plexus, and groin. Note: For safety, this drill must be performed slowly and with extreme caution.

TWELVE

DEFENSES AGAINST A MOUNT

A MOUNT, OR GETTING ON TOP AND STRADDLING AN OPPONENT, OFTEN FOLLOWS

A SUCCESSFUL TAKEDOWN. DEFENSES AGAINST AN ATTACKER MOUNTING YOU

WITH HIS WEIGHT ON TOP OF YOU AND WITH THE ATTACKER'S LEGS STRADDLING

YOU ARE CRITICAL. WHEN TRAINING AGAINST THESE TYPES OF ATTACKS, YOU must think of your fighting chess game and how your attacker will look for a dominant position. Accordingly, you must master a few techniques to avoid being mounted, and especially, having your arms trapped.

MOUNT DEFENSE STRIKES TO THE GROIN

Attack your attacker's groin immediately with punches or downward elbow strikes and then dislodge the attacker from your torso by bucking the attacker. While similar to upper-body defenses, defending strikes from the bottom position of a mount requires you to shift your body weight to not present a fixed target. Never keep your back flat to the ground; always remain slightly raised and on your side to ensure the possibility of movement. Cover your head with forearms, keeping your elbows in to defend against strikes and arm bars, while using body movement by shifting side to side. As you shift when opportune, use a hip buck to dismount the attacker or move to imbalance him. This tactic also sets up a vertical elbow to the attacker's groin and prevents the attacker from gaining the high mount. In summary: (1) cover your head with your forearms to defend and deflect, while (2) combining this defensive tactic with both body defense movement to prevent being a stationary target, while (3) counterstriking simultaneously.

Counterstrike immediately and attempt to bridge by raising your hips to one side with the help of your shoulder facing the direction you hope to launch your attacker. This can be challenging if your attacker carries a considerable weight and strength advantage.

Important strategy: You should never turn facedown and expose the back of your neck to an attacker.

As you strike the attacker in the groin, begin to bridge or raise up on the ball of your right foot to unbalance the attacker. Jolt the attacker forward and to your left corner (the attacker's right corner). Use your arms to create further separation and to jettison the attacker.

Immediately transition to eye gouges to create further separation, allowing you to begin to pivot on your back and place your feet toward the attacker's head.

Kick the attacker in the head with your near-side right leg, using your heel, and begin to get up properly.

Get up by placing your left hand on the ground and withdrawing your right leg backward underneath your torso. Place your weight on both balls of your feet. Keep your right arm up in a defensive position as you rise to your feet.

TOP MOUNT DEFENSE DRILL

This drill requires two partners, P1 (the "Defender" [you]) and P2 ("Attacker" [your partner]). P2 is resting on top of P1's torso simulating a confrontation where P2 initiates as the aggressor performing simulated attacks from the mount. Practitioners should repeat this drill a minimum of 15 repetitions to each side of P1's torso (P2 is ejected to the right and the left with corresponding right and left hand counterattacks) for a mirror drill (30 repetitions total). Finish with retzev continuous ground survival counterattacks as necessary.

This drill should be performed on a mat or padded surface. Against P2's simulated top mount, P1 performs a simulated hammerfist or vertical elbow strike and bucks P2 to the corner. P1 should simulate creating separation and follow up with simulated heel kicks and other attacks to vulnerable anatomy.

Note: For safety, this drill must be performed slowly and with extreme caution.

Additional combatives that you can use when defending the mount include an elbow strike to the groin or eye gouges, if your arms are long enough and the opportunity presents itself. Immediately eject the attacker as demonstrated previously.

THIRTEEN

DEFENDING THE GUARD

WHEN TWO OPPONENTS ARE FIGHTING, THEY MAY CLINCH UP OR GRAB ONE

ANOTHER. THE PHYSICAL CONFRONTATION BECOMES A GRAPPLING STRUGGLE.

ONE OPPONENT MAY FALL BACKWARD TO THE GROUND TO IMMEDIATELY WRAP

HIS LEGS AROUND THE SECOND OPPONENT, PLACING THE SECOND OPPONENT IN the guard position. The guard can be "open" or "closed." An open guard is when one's legs are wrapped around an opponent's torso, but not crossed behind the opponent. A closed guard is when one's legs are wrapped around an opponent's torso with one ankle overlapping the other to lock one's legs around the opponent. For this tactic, you are the person with the attacker's legs wrapped around you. Note: Krav maga does not emphasize using the guard because of its inherent anatomical vulnerabilities (except for some specific military applications).

GROIN STRIKES IF CAUGHT IN THE CLOSED GUARD

If you maintain proper upright body position, the attacker's groin is open to strikes.

Before the attacker can get ahold of any part of you, straighten your back or "posture up" and rudely jam your knee into your attacker's tailbone. This can be a debilitating strike in itself and a counter against your attacker's attempt to control you with his/her legs. Strike your attacker's groin using straight punches, hammerfists, and vertical elbows along with grabs and twists. Be sure to keep your arms close to your torso, as the attacker could trap and secure one of your arms to injure it with an armbar. The high-closed guard can allow your attacker strong body control of you, placing you in a highly vulnerable position.

EYE GOUGES IF THE ATTACKER PULLS YOU INTO HIS CLOSED GUARD

If your attacker successfully breaks your posture and clinches your head, use thumb gouges to the eyes to disengage, followed by retzev.

As the attacker breaks your posture and pulls you in, use your rule of thumbs defense to attack the attacker's eyes. Although you cannot see, simply find the attacker's cheekbones with your palms and immediately jam your thumbs into the attacker's eye sockets.

Upon creating separation, continue your combatives using a knuckle hand strike to the
attacker's throat. Note: This move can seriously damage an opponent and must only
be used if you feel you are in jeopardy of serious injury or if your life is at stake.
Alternatively, if a throat strike is not necessary, punch the attacker in the head.

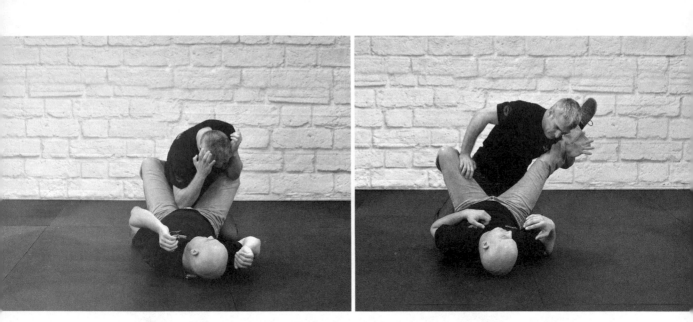

You may also deliver an elbow strike to the attacker's groin instead of a strike to the attacker's throat or a punch. After delivering your successive counterattacks, use your left arm to force the attacker's leg away to your right (the attacker's left).

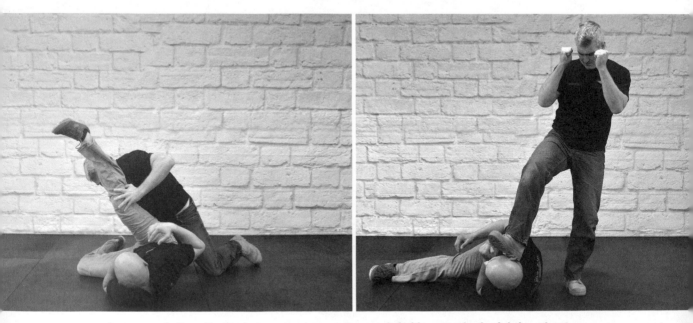

As you push the attacker's leg away, move to your left (the attacker's right) and get up. Deliver a kick to the head or other part of the attacker's body as necessary to end the threat.

GUARD DEFENSE DRILL

This drill requires two partners, P1 (the "Defender" [you]) and P2 ("Attacker" [your partner]). P1 is placed in P2's guard simulating a confrontation where P2 initiates as the aggressor performing simulated attacks from the guard. Practitioners should repeat this drill a minimum of 15 repetitions whereby P1 attacks with the right arm and then with the left arm for a mirror drill (30 repetitions total). Finish with retzev continuous ground survival counterattacks as necessary.

This drill should be performed on a mat or padded surface. Against P2's simulated guard, P1 performs a simulated hammerfist or vertical elbow, striking P2 in the groin. P1 should simulate creating separation, forcing P2's leg to the side, and follow up by immediately standing followed by a simulated stomp.

RESOURCES

For protective padding and other supplies:

Asian World of Martial Arts
9400 Ashton Road
Philadelphia, PA 19114
(800) 345-2962
www.awma.com

Aries Fight Gear
(800) 542-7437
www.punchingbag.com

Mancino Mats
1180 Church Road
Lansdale, PA 19446
(800) 338-6287
www.mancinomats.com

Authentic Israel Army Surplus
P.O. Box 31006
Tel Aviv 61310
Israel
U.S. Local Phone: (718) 701-3955
Toll Free Number: (888) 293-1421
Israel: (972) 3-6204612;
Fax: (972) 9-8859661
www.israelmilitary.com

To read more about krav maga and its history:

Israel Defense Forces
Web site: www.idf.il

Israeli Special Forces Krav Maga
Web site: www.ct707.com

Israeli Krav Maga Association (Gidon System)
Web site: www.israelikrav.com and www.kravmagaisraeli.com

GRANDMASTER HAIM GIDON

Grandmaster Haim Gidon, tenth dan and Israeli Krav Maga Association president, heads Israeli krav maga (Gidon System) from the IKMA's main training center in Netanya, Israel. Haim was a member of krav maga founder Imi Lichtenfeld's first training class in the early 1960s. Along with Imi and other top instructors, Haim Gidon cofounded the IKMA. In 1995, Imi nominated Haim as the top authority to grant first dan krav maga black belts and up. Haim represented krav maga as the head of the system on the professional committee of Israel's National Sports Institute, Wingate. Grandmaster Gidon, whose professional expertise is in worldwide demand, has taught defensive tactics for the last thirty years to Israel's security and military agencies. Grandmaster Haim Gidon is ably assisted by some of the highest ranked and most capable krav maga instructors in the world, which includes Ohad Gidon (sixth dan), Noam Gidon (fifth dan), Yoav Krayn (fifth dan), Yigal Arbiv (fifth dan), and Steve Moishe (fourth dan). More information is available at www.kravmagaisraeli.com.

SENIOR INSTRUCTOR RICK BLITSTEIN

Rick Blitstein is one of a few handpicked individuals who traveled to Netanya, Israel, in 1981 to complete an intensive krav maga instructor course. Under the watchful eye of krav maga founder Imi Lichtenfeld, Israeli experts taught Rick so that Rick could introduce the teachings of krav maga to the United States. Imi and Rick formed very close bonds and spent much time training together in both Israel and the United States. For many of the past thirty years, Rick has worked in the field of private and corporate security, teaching and using krav maga in real-life situations. A member of the IKMA and recognized as a senior black-belt instructor, Rick is committed to the proper expansion of the system in the United States and around the world. Rick sent the author to train with the IKMA for instructor certification. More information is available at www.israeli kravmaga.com.

INSTRUCTOR/PHOTOGRAPHER RINALDO ROSSI

Black-belt instructor Rinaldo Rossi began his krav maga training in 2001 and his advanced training with David Kahn in 2006. Rinaldo completed his instructor certification with Grandmaster Haim Gidon in both the United States and Israel. Rinaldo is one of only a few Americans to complete Grandmaster Gidon's certification course in Israel. Rinaldo has taught at the Marine Corps Martial Arts Center of Excellence (Quantico), a Navy Advanced Training Command, the FBI Academy (Quantico), and the New Jersey State Police Academy. Rinaldo is responsible for the national rollout of Israeli krav maga in the United States with senior instructors Don Melnick and Chris Eckel in coordination with the Israeli Krav Maga Association.

ABOUT THE AUTHOR

David Kahn, IKMA United States Chief Instructor, received his advanced black-belt teaching certifications from Grandmaster Haim Gidon and is the only American to sit on the IKMA board of directors. David was also awarded a fifth-degree black belt in combat jiu-jitsu by the United States Judo Association. He has formally trained all five branches of the U.S. military, the Royal Marines, in addition to federal, state, and local law enforcement agencies in many training-school houses, including Marine Corps Martial Arts Center of Excellence (MACE), Army Combatives School (Fort Benning), a Navy Advanced Training Command, along with those of the FBI, New Jersey State Police, and a host of other academies. David is certified as an instructor by the State of New Jersey Police Training Commission. David has been featured in various media outlets including *Men's Fitness, GQ, USA Today, The Los Angeles Times, The Washington Post, The New Yorker, Penthouse, Fitness, Marine Corps News,* Armed Forces Network, *Special Operations Report,* and Military.com. David is the author of *Krav Maga* (2004), *Advanced Krav Maga* (2008), *Krav Maga Weapon Defenses* (2012), and *Krav Maga Professional Tactics* (2016). He has produced the award-winning *Mastering Krav Maga* DVD series (Volumes I, II, III) and Volume IV, *Mastering Krav Maga: Defending the 12 Most Common Unarmed Attacks,* along with the *Mastering Krav Maga Online* program. David and his partners operate several Israeli krav maga training centers of excellence. For more information contact info@israelikrav.com.

For video of the techniques featured in this book along with the rest of the civilian Israeli krav maga curriculum, the following material is available:

DVDS

Mastering Krav Maga: Defending the 12 Most Common Unarmed Attacks was produced as a companion for *Krav Maga Defense.* Filmed entirely in HD, this eight-disc set (approximately ten hours of filmed material) is designed as a stand-alone, home-study krav maga program for beginner and advanced students alike. This set also catalogs and demonstrates krav maga's twelve most instinctive, effective counterattacks along with more than two dozen bonus hardcore, build-on combatives, including advanced takedowns, throws, chokes, and joint locks. This set supplements the original self-defense DVD set *Mastering Krav Maga Volume I* (adding 120 new tactics/technique variations). The material focuses on the common mistakes practitioners may make—allowing for self-critique and correction. Further included are core firearm defenses (including the most deadly mistakes) and thirty essential strategy slides examining preconflict indicators; avoidance; de-escalation; escape and evasion; and the kravist's mind/body preparation. To purchase, please visit www.amazon.com, www.masteringkravmaga.com, or www.israelikrav.com.

ONLINE (DEVICE ENABLED) TRAINING

Mastering Krav Maga Online includes 330 lessons or more than forty hours of online lessons covering approximately 90% of the krav maga civilian curriculum. Please visit www.masteringkravmaga.com.

Israeli Krav Maga Main U.S. Training Center

860 Highway 206
Bordentown, NJ 08505
(609) 585-MAGA
www.israelikrav.com

Israeli Krav Maga Association (Gidon System)

POB 1103
Netanya, Israel
www.kravmagaisraeli.com